CAMPUS VALUES

Some Considerations

for Collegians

CAMPUS VALUES

Edited by

CHARLES W. HAVICE

The Russell B. Stearns Study
Northeastern University

Charles Scribner's Sons / New York

GREETINGS

What are your thoughts and opinions concerning the issues that our several authors are discussing in this book? All young men and women attending college will be confronted with many of the problems raised here.

The central purpose of this publication is to provide a springboard for discussion and further reflection. It does not attempt to cover all the issues that a student faces on campus. It does not claim to give a thoroughgoing account even of the several subjects included. Certainly it does not presume to give all the answers. Nevertheless, this volume can fulfill important needs. It presents facts. It also unapologetically presents opinions and beliefs. The discerning student is not likely to confuse the two types of contents. He will use them as guides in formulating his own value system.

GILBERT G. MAC DONALD

THE RUSSELL B. STEARNS STUDY

Northeastern University
Boston, Massachusetts

Named in recognition of its generous sponsor, this study was instituted by President Asa S. Knowles in 1962. Mr. Stearns, a member of the Board of Trustees, continues to support the program and to encourage its development on a nationwide level.

In its concern with the ethical and social behavior of youth, the Study has three basic objectives: research, information distribution, and action. Its responsibility is not only to conduct basic research, but also to apply its findings to practical programs. The research information is disseminated to other researchers, to those who work professionally with young people, and to the young people themselves.

The Stearns Study is currently conducting research on a wide range of ethical and social issues. For the most part these research programs involve students at many different types of colleges. Among the factors being studied are the backgrounds and personalities of the students, their religious commitments, the types of colleges they attend, and the value systems of their friends and peers.

This book is one of the results of the study. Joy D. Winkie prepared the first edition, *Stepping Stones or Stumbling Blocks,* which appeared in 1965. Charles W. Havice edited the second edition and chose the present title. This present edition is based on that second edition.

PREFACE

This small volume treats some of the most important topics in the world. They have to do with what it means to be a human in a period of mankind's history when the inquiry is unusually complex and difficult.

Education has been the social institution through which the answers to our central quest for insight into ourselves and the universe traditionally have been given.

It was presumed for centuries that the necessary knowledge for successful living and dying was already possessed by society. The task of the school and the teacher in such a situation was quite clear and straightforward. Despite a minority of doubters, the methodology of simple inculcation was quite useful and appropriate for a long time. And it seems to have worked reasonably well. Mankind has waxed and grown stronger through the ages. Until the recent past!

It seems ironic that, although we now have nearly acquired the keys which will unlock the physical universe, the interior universe of each man must yet be privately explored. The old homilies are no longer acceptable as unquestionably correct merely because they are taught. Statements once offered as absolutes now must be tested frequently in the crucible of personal experience. This new methodology has been the vehicle of scientific progress. It has freed men from purblind acceptance of authoritarian declarations regarding the nature of man and his destiny.

But this new order of the ages has required a price. Into the vacuum left by the removal of old certitudes have returned the primal questions to be treated anew. What does it mean to be human? What is the proper relation of man to man? What do freedom and responsibility mean? How does man relate to the great Unmoved Mover? These and other questions are no longer neatly resolved by aphorisms. Every person must seek many of the answers by his own pursuit of truth.

The task of education has been reformulated so that now it seeks to aid the personal quest, but not to fulfill it wholly. The technique is one of exploration, experimentation, and synthesis in a continuing cycle.

This new mode of operation, however, does not require the setting aside of the accumulated wisdom of the race. Not by any means. Rather, it requires the skillful presentation by teachers of that distillation so that the learner can see it in its clearest light. The voices of reason and prudence may then be heard. Some forms of wisdom do not lend themselves to the scientific method, but must be rationalized or intuitively understood on other bases. That is one of the difficult tasks to which the contributors and the editor of this book have addressed themselves. What they have essayed to do is to present to you in concise form some of the major problems to be met in arriving at full humanity. Set down next to the questions are some answers forged from the thought and experience of many questers who preceded you, as well as from the work of some who are your contemporaries. You must now engage the task in your own unique way.

PHILIP A. TRIPP

ACKNOWLEDGMENTS

Often the editorial *we* is used perfunctorily to dissuade the reader from concluding that the writer's ego is oversized. In this instance, the plural pronoun is used quite literally. The editor cannot possibly express the extent of his debt to the many persons who have cooperated. Together, we have made this publication possible.

To the authors go fullest measures of gratitude for making the book substanstively possible. That each writer has outstanding qualifications will be apparent to the reader. The eagerness with which each author entered into the project added zest to the whole effort.

Mr. Russell B. Stearns has demonstrated his interest in the moral and social behavior of American youth by giving substantial support, personal and financial, of the total project—the Russell B. Stearns Study—of which this book is a part.

President Asa S. Knowles, envisioning the usefulness of such a publication, led us to foresee its possibilities and to set about producing it. His sustained personal interest has reinforced our efforts throughout.

Among colleagues on campus who have given assistance are the following: John S. Bailey, Dean of University College; Richard W. Bishop, Assistant to the President; Philip C. Boyd, Assistant to the President; Carl S. Ell, President Emeritus; Walter L. Fogg, Professor of Philosophy and Religion; Colin B. Gracey, Episcopal Chaplain;

Christopher F. Kennedy, Dean of Freshmen; Frank E. Marsh, Dean of Education; Thomas E. McMahon, Director of Cooperative Education; Robert A. Mize, Catholic Chaplain; Edward W. Robinson, Dean of Men; Kenneth G. Ryder, Dean of Administration; Don Stewart, University Editor; Chester W. Storey, Associate Director of Publications; William C. White, Executive Vice-President; Roy L. Wooldridge, Dean of Cooperative Education. Miss Manola E. Simpson and Miss Helen White gave editorial help.

To acknowledge individually the helpfulness of many friends on other campuses is certain to result in inadvertent omissions. For such oversight the editor alone is culpable. Among those whose counsel has enhanced the Stearns Study generally and this book particularly are the following colleagues: Paul K. Addams, National Interfraternity Conference, New York; Chester M. Alter, chancellor, University of Denver; DeWitt C. Baldwin, University of Michigan; H. Russell Beatty, president, Wentworth Institute; Robert H. Beaven, University of Rochester; Myron B. Bloy, Jr., Massachusetts Institute of Technology; George K. Brown, Carnegie Institute of Technology; John L. Cowan, University of Minnesota; J. Edward Dirks, Danforth Foundation, St. Louis, Missouri; Sidney B. Denman, Stetson University; Frank E. Duddy, Jr., president, Marietta College; Ralph G. Dunlop, Northwestern University; Edward D. Eddy, Jr., president, Chatham College; Luther H. Foster, president, Tuskegee Institute; Samuel L. Gandy, Howard University; Joseph Gluck, West Virginia University; Jeffrey K. Hadden, Western Reserve University; Robert H. Hamill, Boston University; Philip E. Jacob, University of Pennsylvania; Norman B. Johnson, Union College; Stanley H. King, Harvard University; Wilma Smith Leland, St. Paul, Minnesota; James S. Leslie, Ohio Wesleyan University; Ernest M. Ligon, Character Research Project, Union College; Franklin H. Littell, president, Iowa Wesleyan College; Milton D. McLean, Southern Illinois University; Henry Q. Middendorf, Polytechnic Institute of Brooklyn; Clifford A. Nelson, Pennsylvania State University; Theodore M. Newcomb, University of Michigan; Dr. Edward Rackman, Yeshiva University; Paul H. Rahmeier, Dartmouth College; Robert Rankin, Danforth Foundation; John Robson, Menasha, Wisconsin; B.F.D. Runk, University of Virginia; H. George Russell, Pennsylvania State University; Seymour A. Smith, president, Stephens College; Robert V. Smith, Colgate University; Pitirim A. Sorokin, Harvard University; Foster Strong, California Institute of Technology; Kenneth G. Underwood, Wesleyan University; Howard C. Wilkinson, Duke University; Edmund G. Williamson, University of Minnesota; Herman E. Wornom, Religious Education Association, New York; and Victor R. Yanitelli, S.J., president, Saint Peter's College.

Special acknowledgment is given our advisory committee: Director Philip Price, New York University, chairman; Vice-President Mark Barlow, Jr., Cornell University; Dean Robert F. Etheridge, Miami University; Professor James C. McLeod, Northwestern University; Dean Glen T. Nygreen, Hunter College; and Dean Ruth E. Warfel, Mount Holyoke College.

The capabilities of my author-secretary Lillian J. Jermane, the responsibilities borne by Kenneth C. Solano, and the office assistance of Silvija A. Mangulis are to be noted with appreciation.

Finally the perceptive comments given by many students have had no small influence in the preparation of this volume.

C.W.H.

CONTENTS

1 / Nevitt Sanford

AIMS OF COLLEGE EDUCATION

A few years ago a colleague and I attended a reception in an upper-middle class district in one of our large inland cities. A young woman whom we had studied intensively when she was in college was announcing her engagement.[1] It was our hope that we would be able to keep in touch with the students we had known so well, at least for some years after they graduated, and attending a reception seemed a pleasant duty. The home was exactly as it had been described by our subject in her life-history interview—a huge, rambling house built about 1900, located on a shady street with a vast garden and great trees bordering a swimming pool. The home was close enough to the center of town so that most of the other houses on the street had been converted into apartment dwellings. There were approximately 200 guests, representing the social and cultural and artistic elite of the city. It was a lively party.

As we left, it was necessary to wait quite a while for a taxi, and our hostess—our research subject—undertook to fill us in a bit on life in her city. She explained that most of the people that we had met were chronic party-goers, and she took the trouble to single out among the departing guests a number of notorious female alcoholics.

[1] As a part of the Mary Conover Mellon Program at Vassar College; see N. Sanford (ed.), "Personality development during the college years," *Journal of Social Issues,* 1956, *12,* No. 4.

She explained that in this town there was nothing for educated people to do. There was a symphony concert one evening a week, but during the rest of the time people engaged in a round of parties, with heavy drinking the rule. With many of the women, the drinking started with three cocktails before lunch. Then, about three o'clock, one of the group would say, "I have a wonderful idea—let's all go over to my house and have a drink," which they did, and thus whiled away the time until the husbands arrived when they began preparations for going out to dinner. Our informant's fiance, who was from an eastern metropolis, was shocked. It was further explained that at the parties the talk usually focused on gossip and happenings inside the several organizations with which most of the men were identified. Undoubtedly the women of this social group, all of whom were college-educated, had had many occasions to complain about the lack of stimulation in this culturally barren and sociologically depressed community. Depressing is the word. The center of the city revealed no sign of civic pride: shabby public buildings and a continuous snarl of traffic. To go any distance from the center of the city was to pass through vast slums. The delinquency rate would match that of any of our large cities, and the college-educated women of the city were bored and could find nothing to do with themselves.

I first recorded this incident in 1962 and used it as a basis for a critique of our colleges and universities.[2] Where, I asked, was the sense of social responsibility, the capacity to go on learning, the demand for aesthetic and intellectual satisfaction that colleges claimed to encourage. Where was the self-confidence that would enable college graduates to assume some leadership in what seemed a desperate situation; where, indeed, was the sensitivity and social awareness that would tell these women and men that the situation *was* desperate. I called attention to the old saying that the trouble with students is that they turn into alumni.

It will be agreed, I think, that since 1962 our cities have deteriorated even further and that although a new mood of concern and self-doubt is present in our country as a whole, life among the upper-middle class goes on much as before.

Of course it is not fair to place all the blame for this state of

[2] N. Sanford, "Higher education as a social problem." In N. Sanford (ed.), *The American College* (New York, 1962), pp. 10–11. I have here paraphrased what was said in that volume.

affairs upon the colleges. It can be said that no matter what the colleges do students will still "turn into alumni," that is to say, they will return to main street, where they will be under heavy pressure to conform with the prevailing values and standards of conduct. But where, if not to the colleges and their students, are we to look for the will and the knowledge to improve matters? Colleges and their students are bound to reflect and to be shaped by the society of which they are parts but no one doubts that they have a major responsibility for the quality of life in our country today.

It must be said also that sometimes colleges do have a deep and lasting influence on their students. Our informant, the young woman who was planning to be married, is a case in point. She was able to see what was going on. She was able to view the whole scene in a perspective she had acquired in college, offering an analysis of it that seemed both compassionate and sociologically accurate, and revealing values and tastes according to which it could be properly evaluated. It is a fairly safe bet, too, that her new orientation has endured, partly because she was marrying a man who shared her outlook and interests.

One might hope that colleges could have this kind of impact more often. If they did they would go a long way toward overcoming the kind of personal and social failure that my story illustrates. If a majority of the opinion makers, or the "power structure" of our inland city had developed as our informant did the whole atmosphere of the place would be different. The college-educated would have the inner resources to assure that they would never be bored, they would have the capacity to create the high culture necessary to satisfy their aesthetic and intellectual needs, and they would have the inclination to improve the lot of their neighbors. But more than this would be needed in order to transform this metropolis in a favorable way. Much knowledge and wisdom would be needed. We are speaking here of social and cultural change, and to do this is to raise questions about the directions and ends of change. Answers are not likely to be found by asking the man in the street or by looking to the prevailing ways of particular social classes or subcultures; we have to look instead to our colleges and universities where the great ideas of world civilization are preserved and interpreted and made useable, where knowledge of present possibilities is discovered and disseminated, and where students and their teachers can on this basis develop visions of the future. When it was decided in this way what to do there would remain the question of how to do it—how to bring about desired change in society and how to produce the goods and supply the services necessary to satisfy human needs.

Implicit in what I have just said are three major goals of education; or one might say *the* three major aims: the development of the individual, the preservation and advancement of culture, and the maintenance and further development of technology. There are various other goals as we shall see, but virtually all of any importance can be brought under one or another of these headings.

I am going to argue that these three goals are interrelated, but that the goal of individual development is supreme. It is an ultimate value. If we ask what is a good society the answer, for me, is that it is the kind of society that is best for man, which is to say the kind that enables him to become all he is capable of becoming. At the same time, individual development favors and is often a necessary condition for the attainment of the other goals.

Individual development owes much to culture which each person assimilates in his own way, but the preservation and further enrichment of culture depends most heavily upon developed individuals. Individual development may also be furthered by vocational training, which may expand the individual's abilities and help him to define himself at a time when this is needed, but it is only the developed individual who can adapt himself creatively and productively to the rapidly changing requirements of the world of work. In sum, it is through psychological development that we may discover and maintain our humanity, participate fully in the benefits of a complex culture, and be truly useful to society.

Of the various ways in which a person can be useful to society, one of the most important is through a vocation or profession; and in our society accomplishment in this sphere is well rewarded, both materially and psychologically. Thus it is common for people to say that one goes to college so that he will be able to "get a good job," which will be the means by which he can go up in the world or at least maintain the status he has already. A student's parents, relatives, and friends are likely to put pressure on him to say what "he is going to do," treating something that is practically important as if it were a moral imperative. By entering a vocation or a profession a person may contribute either to culture or to technology, or to both. In any case, his preparation must include a considerable amount of specialized *training*. Thus a distinction is often made between "vocational education" or "professional education," which prepares a person for his job, and "liberal" or "general" education, which inducts him into the life and spirit of his culture and develops him as a person. (When I was in college we tried to keep our anxiety in check by debating whether the purpose of it all was to "earn a living" or to learn "how to live," coming down on one or the other side of the question depending on the degree of our certainty about what we were "going to do.") I think it is helpful to distinguish between *education* and *training*. Education is the educing of whatever potential lies within the individual. It is by definition, in other words, a deliberate effort to further individual development. Education is liberating and differentiating, and if it is successful it makes every individual different from every other. Training, on the other hand, tends to process individuals so that they become more alike, speaking the same special language and engaging in the same kinds of activities in nearly the same prescribed way. As I have indicated, education and training may go on at the same time and interact to their mutual benefit, but, in general, education should come first and training should be postponed as long as is practicable. This is not only because training goes along better and faster when the person has been educated but also because settling prematurely upon a vocation and opening oneself to the processes of the training for it may put serious obstacles in the way of further development; it may restrict one's vision of what he might become and cut one off from enlarging experiences.

In this light it seems regrettable that so many over-ambitious middle-class parents seem willing to stake everything upon their children's early decision for a particular career, and that opinion generally in this country holds that lower-class young people must learn a trade before anything good can happen to them. In this last situation there is involved more than a wrong-headed notion about education; there is a mean-spirited carry-over from our puritan heritage which holds that these young people must learn a trade and work at it in order to *deserve* the benefits of full participation in our society. It is all right, according to this view, for middle-class young people to bide their time for four years in the halls of ivy, "discovering their identity," "learning how to get along with people," developing tastes for this or that aspect of high culture and so on; they deserve it by virtue of having had the right parents and, anyway, their college activities can be called "work"; but lower-class youngsters must be seen as constituting a "manpower problem" which is to be solved by all kinds of training and retraining programs and by massive schemes for the allocation of jobs.

I am not complaining because middle-class college students have it so good; I think everybody should have it as good and that we as a nation can easily afford it. It is not that everybody has the ability to do what is called "college work," but everybody can be educated in my sense of the word; each individual can be developed to a level that will permit him to participate with enjoyment in what our culture has to offer. The thing to do for people who are not likely to find jobs in our increasingly automated technology is to educate them. We should do this because we are an enlightened and humane people. But if by this course we succeed in arousing "motivation for work" in lower-class youngsters, who often believe they will be out of it no matter what they do, so much the better.

Now, in order to make my case for individual development I must say what it is. I must specify some of its goals, indicate how it occurs, and show that it can take place in college as well as at various other times of life. Then I shall undertake to show that although it is advantageous to state educational aims in the terms of modern personality theory (it helps us to plan for their realization), my general philosophy has a long tradition behind it, having been espoused by the Ancients and by the Founding Fathers. Before concluding with some remarks about obstacles in the way of the achievement of our highest aims, obstacles not the least of which are the conflicting, short-term aims of various people, including some educators, who have an interest in the matter, I shall argue that only developmental education can prepare the student for the world he is about to enter.

PERSONALITY DEVELOPMENT

It is common sense to observe a person over a period of time, to note that he is consistently aggressive or dominant or submissive, and to think of personality as the aggregate of *traits* such as these.

It is also common sense to think of personality as what is referred to when a person uses the pronoun "I." Both of these conceptions have much in common with, but neither is the same thing as, personality as it is defined by most specialists in the field. Not all consistency of behavior can be ascribed to personality. The characteristic aggressiveness of a person, for example, may be due not so much to a persisting disposition of personality as to the fact that the person is constantly in a situation so frustrating as to evoke aggressive behavior in anyone. Personality, in its most widely accepted technical sense, refers to dispositions *in the person* that help to determine behavior and that differ from one person to another. There may be durable dispositions in a person that determine some of his behavior but do not enter into his awareness, either because he is unwilling to admit their existence or because he is unable to formulate them for himself.

What are the dispositions of personality, and how are they organized? One approach to these questions that has proved useful in the past and that can serve our present purpose conceives of the personality as comprising three major systems: a system of primitive impulses and feelings; a system of inhibiting or punishing forces that have been automatically taken over from the social environment (the primitive conscience); and a system of forces that operates in accord with the demands of reality which controls impulses and feelings and integrates both of the preceding systems with itself. The inner life of the person consists largely in conflicts and alliances among these systems and it is to patterns of their interaction that we may largely attribute observable traits of personality. Impulses are often in conflict with the demands of conscience, and the ego has the task of finding, for impulses, modes of gratification that are acceptable to conscience and in keeping with the requirements of reality. Anxiety, doubt, guilt, or behavior that is restricted or peculiar attend the ego's failures; satisfaction and joy attend its success.

Growth may be defined simply as expansion—the addition of features and the enlargement of different ones. For example, with increasing age the child acquires more needs and some of the needs that he has increase in intensity. Development means, most essentially, the organization of complexities which increase in number and magnitude. For example, a child behaves in an all-or-nothing fashion because his personality is very much all of one piece; with time, various sub-systems become differentiated and take on particular functions; and without losing their particular identity, these subsystems become integrated into larger wholes in order to serve the larger purposes of the organism.

Using the terms introduced above to stand for the major systems of the personality, one may say that in the highly developed person there is a rich and varied impulse life, many different impulses having now found various modes of expression. Conscience has been broadened and refined in the sense that it is sensitive to many different kinds of moral issues, and, having been brought under the sway of the ego's processes, it operates in accord with the person's best thought and judgment. The ego has at its disposal a wide range of sensibilities and adaptive capacities; it may judge events and control actions in accord with reality while remaining in close enough touch with impulses that may be expressed in many culturally sanctioned ways.

Growth occurs mainly in response to graded challenges. A child comes into the world with natural susceptibilities to tension; internal or external stimuli immediately arrive to make tension actual (to arouse, in other words, a need or drive) and thus to induce striving. Unless the child's need is immediately taken care of by other people, the striving will continue until he has found some other means of reducing tension. With repetition of the stimuli and of successful striving, the child will soon show an inclination to use the objects and patterns of action that served him. He has now grown, for the personality contains a "need-image-of-object" and a "need-pattern-of-action" that it did not contain before. The child would no doubt be content to go on using his new-found patterns; but it soon turns out that they are not adequate to new stimuli and tension states, and thus the whole chain of events begins again.

It is the growth of the personality that makes development necessary. Just as a social organization like a business or educational institution cannot exceed a certain size without breaking into smaller sections and developing a more complex structure of control and administration, so a personality cannot expand beyond certain limits without increasing in complexity. Different functions have to be assigned to different parts; channels of communication among the parts have to be set up; and diverse activities have to be coordinated or brought together in larger units.

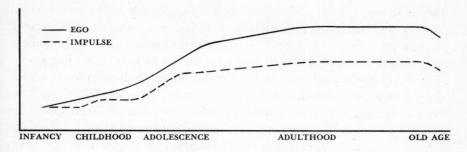

*Development of the ego and of impulse
according to dynamic theory of personality.*

The principles of growth and development that hold for childhood hold also for the adolescent years and afterwards. Because of their greater repertory of routine responses, adolescents and adults do not change as readily as children, but these older people will change when confronted with stimuli that cause instability they cannot correct with their existing modes of adaptation.

Several important statements about development can be made on the basis of the curves shown in the figure which have been drawn largely on the basis of theory but are not inconsistent with information now available. Note that both impulse and ego continue to grow in strength through college and well into adulthood. The reason adults do not as a rule develop very much is because they are able to arrange their lives in such a way that they are sufficiently rewarded and inefficiently challenged. Let an adult embark on some new mode of existence—for example, let him retire after holding a position for a long time—and he will, provided he is pretty well developed already, exhibit a developmental spurt, marked by new interests and a whole range of new capacities for response. For that matter, people can still develop on their death beds, by facing reality and deriving new meanings from their experiences. There is no denying, alas, that both impulse and ego finally taper off, but it should be remarked for the benefit of college freshmen in particular that this tapering off occurs later than they are apt to think. Someone asked an 80 year old grandmother when a woman became too old for romance. She of course answered that she didn't know!

It is to be noted also that the relations of impulse and ego are different at different periods of life. The curves have been drawn in such a way as to indicate that impulse is actually in the ascendancy at the beginning, and that it approaches this state at later times, around the age of four or five when the child's "family romance" is at its height and again during the "storm and stress" of adolescence. The striking thing about the freshman's stage of development is that the maximum crisis of adolescence is over, and controlling mechanisms are again in the ascendancy. But the controls developed for the purpose of inhibiting impulse are still unseasoned and uncertain; they are likely to operate in a rigid manner, that is, to be rather overdone, as if the danger of their giving way altogether were still very real. The achievement of flexible control, an arrangement in which there is genuine freedom of impulses because there is little danger of their getting out of hand, still lies ahead. Nevertheless impulses are now inhibited or contained with sufficient effectiveness so that the young person can turn his attention to other matters. He is now ready to concentrate upon his relations with the external world, to improve his understanding of that world, and to find a place within it.

This picture of the typical freshman's psychological situation is essentially a picture of an authoritarian personality structure. Authoritarianism in personality is a particular pattern of relationships among impulse, conscience and ego.[3] It is a pattern in which strong impulses are directly opposed by an alert, rigid, and punitive conscience. The ego has to devote so much energy to restraining impulses that its other functions are not well performed; it has been able to integrate little of the primitive conscience with itself, so that the latter continues to function more or less as a foreign body. This state of affairs at the core of the personality is reflected at the surface in characteristic ways: in stereotyped thinking, intolerance of ambiguity, punitive morality, submissiveness toward the powerful and dominance toward the weak, conventionality, anti-intellectualism, or hostility toward people perceived to be different from oneself. Authoritarianism can be thought of as a stage of development through which we all go, and at which some of us become fixated. The fact that a majority of Americans seem not to want racial integration can be attributed mainly to the failure of their education to overcome their authoritarian tendencies.

If the young person is not to remain in an authoritarian stage

---

[3] See T. Adorno, Else Frenkel-Brunswik, D. Levinson, and N. Sanford, *The Authoritarian Personality* (New York, 1950), or the paperback edition (New York: John Wiley & Sons, Inc., 1964).

of development and go on naively participating in and becoming blind to or even identified with the prevalent moral shortcomings of our society, he must learn to see things as they are, to develop an articulate individual power of judgment, and become able to criticize what he judges to be bad. Now, however, he courts new danger: that he will reject the existing order out of hand, and become totally alienated from the society and value system represented by his parents and his community.

There is evidence that this has been happening with increasing frequency in recent years, thus posing for educators a new kind of educational task. But popular writing has greatly overestimated the proportion of students who take this course and often mis-classified those students who, with much enthusiasm, become active in the interests of improving their educational institutions and the larger society. The great mass of college freshmen still need to be liberated, and this is the big challenge to educators.

Happily, I am able to report on the basis of a great deal of recent research that authoritarianism generally declines in students who go through four year liberal arts programs.[4] The decline is relatively sharp during the first two years, less so during the second two. As to what happens to students who are like those who figured in the research but who do not go to college nothing is known, but we do know that students who complete some kinds of programs in some kinds of institutions, non-liberal arts programs in a large metropolitan university, for example, are not likely to change in authoritarianism. Thus we may presume that college can make a difference.

A decline in authoritarianism is in keeping with the general theory of personality development outlined above; and so is the finding that, in general, impulses become freed, through being brought under flexible control, as students go through college.

We are speaking here of mean differences in personality scale scores between freshmen and seniors. These differences are statistically significant and they have turned up in more than a few colleges, but they are not really large differences; the fact remains that many students go through four years of college with virtually no change

4 See, for example, in N. Sanford (ed.), *The American College* (New York, 1962), H. Webster, M. Freedman, and P. Heist "Personality changes in college students," and H. A. Korn "Personality scale changes from freshman to the senior year." Also J. Katz (ed.), *Growth and Constraint in College Students* (Stanford, Calif., Institute for the Study of Human Problems, 1967).

in these personality attributes and some students actually become more authoritarian. Nevertheless, it is clear that these and various other attributes of personality *can* change in a favorable way in college, sometimes with the result that the whole direction of a student's life is changed. We must then raise the question: How can favorable changes be produced in more students and in a greater degree?

In answer, I should say that the first step is for educators and students and those who foot the bills for education to become devoted to the idea that individual development really is the over-riding goal of college education. It is an idea that has been stated eloquently, though not always to a receptive audience, from time to time throughout the whole history of western civilization, and fresh arguments in its support can be developed today through a consideration of the demands of life in the modern world.

In 1947, President Truman's Commission on Higher Education released a report which stated

To liberate and perfect the intrinsic power of every citizen is the central purpose of democracy; and its furtherance of individual self-realization is its greatest glory. . . . The first goal in education for democracy is the full, rounded, and continuing development of the person.

This Commission had, I think, captured something of the spirit of the Founding Fathers; and they had almost certainly taken note of the writings of Alfred North Whitehead who wrote, "Students are alive, and the purpose of education is to stimulate and guide their self-development."[5] For my part, when I have wanted in this present connection something useable from the past I have found nothing that suited me better than Alexander Meiklejohn's book *What Does America Mean?* Here this great philosopher, college president, and educational innovator develops the idea that what America is really about is embodied in two simple gifts of counsel: Socrates' "Know thyself" and Jesus' "Love thy neighbor as thyself." All the goals of individual development that were stated above can be condensed into these two statements. Yet we still need a personality theory to help clarify these lofty ideals, to permit us to see their interrelations and the ways in which they depend upon educational policies and procedures.

Our love of our neighbor, to take an example, increases with our knowledge of him, so we teach anthropology and arrange for contacts

[5] A. N. Whitehead, *The Aims of Education* (New York, 1959).

with different cultures. But it also depends on our knowledge of ourselves, for if we are blind to our own weaknesses and aggressive impulses we may easily attribute them to our neighbor and make them grounds for hating him, so we strive to overcome authoritarianism. Our love of our neighbor also depends on our love of ourselves, love in the sense of respect and acceptance, for self-contempt and self-doubt make us selfish and egotistical and unable to give anything to a neighbor. This is why we seek to liberate impulses through building flexible controls. But to know ourselves we must be loved by others, otherwise we would lack the confidence that self-examination requires. And to love ourselves with full knowledge of ourselves we need to be regarded with understanding and compassion. We try then to make a college a genuinely human community. It follows from this that when we love our neighbor we help *him* to achieve self-knowledge.

Only a well developed individual can meet the challenges being posed today by changes in technology, politics, and society. In the world of work, automation is transforming or eliminating occupational roles. Jobs at the unskilled and technical levels disappear first, but even in the professions few are doing what they were trained to do. Instead of educating people for particular roles therefore we must try to provide adaptable intellectual tools and ways of approaching problems that will serve in a diversity of situations, and we must develop in students the flexibility that will enable them to go on learning and to maintain a stable sense of themselves through a succession of changing roles.

In our highly complex systems of business and government, even of professional and academic life, each role is meshed with so many others that individuality is difficult to sustain. If a person involved in this vast machinery is to find satisfaction in his work he must have the breadth to see his productive role in perspective. If he is to maintain his personality he must be able to see himself as existing independently of the organization, and have something inside himself that will support his values against organizational pressures.

He must also have an education general enough so that he can lead a meaningful life apart from his occupation. A man can no longer define himself just in terms of his occupational role. He is also a father, an educator, a committeeman, a citizen, and probably, if he is in the middle class, an all around do-it-yourself man. If he is to take these different roles comfortably, without feeling that his status is being lowered or his masculinity impaired, he must have a flexible self-conception based on familiarity with many aspects of his own personality.

As the standard of living goes up, the role of consumer becomes more central to people's lives. What they choose to consume will determine the level of taste in our culture. If it is to be enhanced or even maintained, higher education must produce increasing numbers of sensitive and discriminating persons.

Most important, education can help to restore the responsible individual who is vanishing into a tangle of organized social roles and group memberships. Contemplating vast and complex social processes, a student may ask poignantly, "What can one person do?" Education must give him insight into how our system works, and how it poses threats to individual freedom; it must somehow, despite the overpowering social pressures on individuals, give him, or help him to maintain, a sense of himself.

The wars, both "cold" and "hot," have led to moral deterioration in our national life. Strident voices have been demanding that we ought to fight fire with fire, and it seems to be more or less official policy that any means are justified so long as they are believed to contribute to the defeat of Communism and that brutality is to be regarded as a necessary, even an ordinary, part of modern life. If we hope to counter these authoritarian tendencies in our national life, if we look toward the day when apathy is replaced by a widespread sense of social responsibility, then students must learn how to ask hard questions, to discuss them without fear and to move beyond ideas that are no longer relevant.

In the shrinking world of today there is no place for tribalism, and the person who regards himself as categorically different from people of other national, ethnic, or social groups is living in the past and is a threat to civic and world peace. We must seek to develop in the student the capacity to look upon other people, all other kinds of people, and feel that they share with him a common humanity. To become a true citizen of the world, an individual must be at home with himself, and be able to include within his conscious scheme of things his deeper emotional dispositions. Education can and must help students to achieve this integration of personality.[6]

[6] All of these ideas about the demands of life in the modern world have been discussed at greater length in my book *Where Colleges Fail* (San Francisco: Jossey-Bass, 1967). What is offered here is an abridgement of that discussion.

In recent years students have been showing a great deal of interest in their own development. For example, in a national survey just completed by the American Council on Education, entering freshmen were asked to consider a list of 18 educational objectives and to check the essential or very important ones. Eighty-six per cent checked "Develop a philosophy of life." Next in order of importance was "Be an authority in my field" (71%); then came "Help others in difficulty" (60%) and "Keep up with political affairs" (57%).

Entering students should not expect, however, that their interest in developmental education will be shared by all the teachers and officials at their institution, or even that their interest in helping other people and becoming involved in current affairs will be understood by many. Universities have other functions besides teaching, and among these, research, training, and public service—with priorities in this last being determined according to the conventional wisdom—receive the lion's share of public support. Colleges, particularly the highly selective colleges, are heavily influenced by what the universities do. Teachers in both kinds of institutions had rather teach subjects than students. They have a deep interest in what is going on at the frontiers of their fields, but high success in their careers depends upon their becoming known as authorities in their disciplines. More than this, college administrators have to pay attention to the interests of other people besides students; parents, alumni, rich donors, state legislators, and the man in the street are likely to let it be known that they consider it far more important that a student prepare for a job, find his place in the existing society, and adhere to conventional moral standards than that he develop his own philosophy of life.

But students will find plenty of support in most colleges for their desire to "become an authority in a field of knowledge." This by itself is enough to make it possible for a resourceful and determined student to develop himself in college. Of all the resources that a college has to offer, the curriculum or the intellectual fare is the most important for personality development. It is through his contact with ideas, with the content of academic learning, that a student may develop his own "technology," i.e., the means for achieving all kinds of practical ends, and his own "culture," i.e., the system of values, symbols, and ideas that enables him to find in vicarious living, imaginative participation in art and literature and all kinds of creative endeavor, the means for expressing his deepest emotional impulses and for satisfying his distinctively human needs, to find meaning, to resolve inner conflicts, to express personality. A student may extend his Self through becoming identified with disciplined work, loving his work as he loves himself, the way a professor becomes involved in his specialty, and he may expand the world of his affections by learning to love ideas and arrangements of ideas in the same way that he loves objects and people.

The curriculum may be presented in an unattractive way; the system of courses, units, and grades may be more than a little annoying; but the material is *there*, to be discovered and integrated with the personality.

Of course, the kind of development we have been talking about depends not only upon the curriculum but upon the whole educational environment. To overcome authoritarianism and to become an independent thinker, for example, a student needs more than the kind of involvement with ideas that I have just described; he needs practice in criticism and the self-esteem and confidence that will enable him to stand in opposition to pressures of authority and of the immediate social group. He also needs models of independent thinking, a general climate of freedom in his college, and a rule structure that is appropriate to his stage of development. The time will come when all this will be well understood by educators, who will then use all the resources of the college in furthering developmental education, guiding their actions by knowledge of how students actually develop.

2 / *Walter D. Wagoner*

THE CAMPUS AND THE GENERATION GAP

The worst mother-in-law story I know is this: a man and his mother-in-law were on a ship to Europe. A storm sank the ship. The man was rescued by the United States Coast Guard. His mother-in-law was lost at sea. The Coast Guard took the man's address in Chicago and advised him that should they find the body they would send a telegram. A week later the wire arrived: "Mother-in-law's body found on New Jersey Coast covered with lobsters. Please instruct." The son-in-law wired back: "Send lobsters to Chicago and reset bait!" I mention this ghoulish story because it is the kind of hard truth that most of us admit only to psychiatrists: namely, that there are many occasions in life when we feel genuine hostility toward those whom we genuinely love—mothers, fathers, sisters, as well as mothers-in-law. And the thing works both ways. Parents, despite their basic love for children, have moments when they would gladly dump them up to their necks in the nearest swamp. There is no use denying these feelings or hiding them behind molasses-covered double-talk. We reach a certain maturity when we are able to accept these hostilities in ourselves and others, take them in stride and in perspective, and not let them cripple our ability to love those whom we occasionally dislike.

All of this is preface to noting that for many people, both parents and college-bound children alike, this ambivalent love-hostility shows itself peculiarly during the college years. For the freshman it may be the hour so long awaited when he or she is finally able to cast off the ropes and row with both oars without a parent at the tiller. And it is a confusing emotion for the collegian to want to thumb his nose at his parents at the very same moment when he wishes to tell them that he loves them very much and will miss them. For the parent there is also the double emotion of relief and regret: glad to get the demanding body out of the house; painfully upset at the absence.

THE GAP INCREASES WITH GEOMETRIC SPEED

The inner tensions so far mentioned are nothing new. They have plagued each generation of college students and their parents. In our day, however, there are some variations on these tensions which are remarkable in the degree of their intensity, even though not completely new. For example, there is the maddening fact that the distance between the generations now seems to be increasing at a geometric rate of speed. My father, so to speak, could shake hands with his father with very little difficulty and over very little distance. They shared much the same outlook on life, the same values, the same economic and political assumptions. What differences they had were largely those of the inevitable stress and strain between any father and son. (My father graduated from college in 1913.) But by the time I graduated from college (1941) this generation-gap was wider than before. A World War, and particularly the Great Depression of the 1930's with its many new social and political measures, profoundly changed the landscape of my boyhood world and made it quite different from that of both my father and his father. New values and different world-views made it, I am certain, much more difficult for me and my father to shake hands. Despite our mutual affection, it was a different world, and I was reading a different road map . . . a map which I for the most part found in college. Today (and my own son graduated from college in 1965), this generation-gap is markedly greater. It takes all of the patience and imagination each generation has in order to find common ground for communication. Again, it is not so much a matter of love or affection as it is of different life styles, new social and political issues, another World War, and the Atomic Age, and a very fast-moving change in rules of the road—a change occurring geometrically, not arithmetically. And these symbols are revealing: my grandfather grew up in the horse and buggy age; my father, in the Model T era; I was raised on "45 mile per hour expressways"! My son flew across the United States in a jet before he crossed it in a car. Now it is culture a-go-go. This generation-gap, in a highly mobile culture where families move often and in which fathers travel much, in a world of staggering problems, creates real psychic, familial, and cultural strain. The college years permit this strain to come out in the open. It is very upsetting to both generations when the old securities, common assumptions, etc., are stretched to the breaking point. Just what and where are "the ties that bind"?

THE TIDY WORLD IS NO MORE

There is another side to this generation-gap which is worth a more detailed sketch. There is a massive dislocation of the old sub-cultures. By sub-cultures I refer loosely to those interlocking institutions, folkways and mores in which we are reared. My own sub-culture happened to be the W.A.S.P. affair—White Anglo-Saxon Protestant. We each come out of some such sub-culture: it may have been Catholic parochial schools, or Jewish in-groups, or a pocket of agnostic free-thinkers. My own sub-culture had its web of friends, summer camps, predictable routines, commonly accepted values. It was the kind of America for which the *Reader's Digest* nostalgically longs—the little white church in the vale, with earnest, thrifty Horatio Alger as deacon. We were umbilically plugged into these pre-college sub-cultures. They were delightfully supportive and protective, just one step above a ghetto. But for better or worse, on every campus in the country, these sub-cultures are going snap, crackle, and pop. Whether Republican or Democrat, Christian or Jew, middle or upper class, the college student definitely is eager to burst out of such pre-determined boundaries. He tends to look back on them, not with nostalgia, but with irritation . . . feeling that he has been trapped too long in too narrow a world. The yeasty plural-ism, the instant internationalism, the heterogeneous secularism, the educational escalation, the communications revolution: these have cracked up the old houses in which we and our families grew up. No one is going to put them together again: neither the Old Guard nor the New Frontier. Things have busted wide open . . . politically, morally, religiously. Anyone who wants a tidy world with neat categories and comfortable reflexes will not, by and large, find it on a college campus. The trouble with such a situation is that it, understandably, increases the degree of difficulty in achieving understanding and empathy between parents and college-age children. The parents have to realize that this wide-open world is not only exciting (and terrifying) in its own right but that it is the world of the next generation. The children have to realize that their world will be terribly empty if they permit it to cancel out affectionate rapport with the parental generation.

MORAL OUTRAGE ON CAMPUS

One other very noticeable and strong minority phenomenon on college campuses today is also related to the generation-gap. It is the high decibel level of moral outrage among many college students. I have no idea how long it will last, or how soon it will sour into cynicism or decline into apathy, but all the readings in my work reveal a college generation which is as morally sensitive as it is exasperated. These feelings may be displayed in awkward and jejune, even bizarre and beatnik fashions. But they are real and, on the whole, to be prized as one of our most precious national assets.

What makes this morality so hard to take for many in the older generation is not only its noisy exhibitionism (often verging on an institutionalized adolescence) but the head-on collision it brings with the American Way of Life. We have tended to put that phrase in capital letters, as if it were some sort of religious cult. Our enthusiasm for its finer ingredients may be just the emotion that will inhibit our appreciation, or at least our understanding, of the devastating moral criticism of American*ism* so obvious among college students. It is essentially to be understood, I believe, as a bitter reaction to our national hypocrisies: in race relations, in foreign affairs, in all the double-talk that goes with a society busy rationalizing affluence. Reinhold Niebuhr has dissected these pretenses. George Kennan has pointed to them in our diplomatic history. The contemporary student's sullenness about Vietnam is very much a part of this syndrome. These students simply will not buy pictures of the United States as moralizer and savior of mankind. They find themselves in a culture, furthermore, which likes to think ethically in black and white, good guys and bad buys. They see a culture which aspires to "his and her airplanes" in a starving world. The point need not be labored sermonically. Indeed, the most characteristic feature of student moralizing is that it is so overt, sermon-like. It is a generation which in its mature moments (as it counts maturity) sits around strumming "Eve of Destruction" and which in its more adolescent moments retreats to James Bond and *Playboy*.

The present college generation has a significant minority of persons willing to express their moral restlessness in action: demonstrations, voter registration, Peace Corps, etc. Insofar as this moral restlessness is conjoined with anxieties and insecurities produced by a terrifying world, this generation finds it very difficult to identify with older persons, older symbols, older myths. This lack of identification may be expressed in overt hostility and/or highly angular behavior, dress, and studied "coolness."

This sense of outrage about life means that these students have few or no heroes in the usual sense. To them the churches look like great hothouses intended to grow something called "religion." Colleges may appear to them to be merit-badge machines. Our sexual codes (the ones *we* wish *they* would profess) are hardly persuasive in a sexually titillating society.

ANXIETY AND DAILY CRISIS

With so much going on so fast it is only to be expected that there is anxiety and enough to spare among college students today. The students understand readily enough and painfully enough that their interior world is a viscous mixture of anxiety, fear, and hope—all scrambled together; the hope compounding the anxiety by creating goals which the student fears an over-populated, over-armed world may not permit him to achieve. There is a place in the personal, psychological makeup of humans comparable to the concept of marginal return—that point beyond which we cannot function healthily because the mental burdens we carry outweigh the diminishing strength of our bodies and minds. For how many years can sensitive young men and women be subjected to the worldly confusions, the atomic eschaton, the military demands, and vocational hazards of our kind of world and *not* show severe signs of aberrant behavior?

Growing up, securing independence, finding by trial and error the satisfactions of normal life: this is enough for most of us. But add to that the constant headaches of the world, the daily crises, and we must expect grievous psychosomatic battle scars. At the moment, human resiliency and youthful strength being what they are, this is still a manageable load . . . though there are definite indications of weakening. One does not have to be a psychoanalyst to sense in and behind the statements and lives of students an enormous load of anxiety and worry.

AMBIVALENCE CONCERNING RELIGION

Finally, the heavy stresses and strains of the generation-gap produce marked religious changes. Elsewhere in this book various aspects of one's religious growth (or decline) during college years are discussed. Here I would only remark that, to a rather singular degree, only a minority of students feel comfortable with the word "religion." It is a generation of religious ambivalence. Whereas thirty years ago such ambivalence was often a pendulum swing between church practice and church absence, today it tends to be an ambivalence oscillating between a wistful interest in theology and a profound disenchantment with anything remotely religious. Chaplains and ministers with an affinity for the student mind, capable of presenting good theology, religion and the arts, etc., have a fighting chance. Students will evidence an admiration for those outspoken religionists who are in the forefront of race relations and social-action movements in society. But, in the face of the pervasive secularism of the world, and the suffering in the world, neither church, chaplain, nor minister will get the time of day from students who see only blandness and *status quo ante* in a faith.

The reaction away from religion is seen in the acidic criticism of conventional parish forms where, as one student put it, "we sit smug-simple in salvation and let the Word shuffle by like some broken down nag, an honored campaigner on whom I will most definitely not lay my last two holy dollars . . . in a town where none but the white, right and wealthy abide." What these students want is a sense of urgency, relevancy, excitement, prophetic abrasiveness, agitation. These students cannot abide those of us who wrap our faith like a cultural garment around our necks. They have a more certain instinct for the sword of Christ than for His peace.

Such students are not militantly anti-clerical or anti-church; rather, finding the church and the ministry too boring, they simply get up and tiptoe away from the church. This is much more dangerous than open opposition.

In any event, most of these students are not so much deeply animated by faith as tantalized by it; not so much counting themselves disciples as God-fearers in the outer court; on the whole more adversely critical of than sympathetic with the inherited forms of church life. In those circumstances where our faith is a "causative factor of student unrest" we can be grateful; in those situations where its blandness causes no reaction we should be worried.

3 / *Herbert H. Stroup*

ADVENTURING IN SOCIAL MATURITY

Ages ago that prototype of the human race, Abraham, went out from Ur of the Chaldees "not knowing whither he went" to a place he was to receive as an inheritance. Ulysses, the ancient Greek wanderer, left Ithaca for a life of travel through strange and threatening lands. These heroes of the past point in the present to the situation that faces every young person. Going to college is for many the start of a journey. Adventuring in social maturity constitutes one of the significant opportunities of the college campus years.

The student seeking social maturity must necessarily relate himself effectively to two interrelated features of a college. First, the college is a complex social organization which requires some skill on the part of the student in making his way within it. Happily for the student, many social institutions, including most high schools, with which he has been associated also are complex; thus, he has a basis for familiarity with the nature of a college.

Colleges, whether small or large in student population, are socially complex organizations. Today the student must be knowledgeable of the workings of the highly complex social system on campus and be efficient in meeting its requirements to some degree. A college is composed of a complex group of specialists: trustees, administrators, faculty, students, custodial workers, librarians, graduate assistants, and others. The student needs to know about these specialists and the way in which their very presence orders his personal life. The college makes these specialists available to its students. But the student must have some understanding of their availability and of their skills. The college, through bulletins, orientation programs and other means, seeks to inform students of their opportunities. In the final analysis, however, it is the student himself who must take the initiative to utilize the available specialists. They can be of great help in many ways to a student, but in general they wait upon him.

Similarly, the college by its bureaucratic nature is composed of a seemingly endless variety of traditions, rules and regulations, cultural expectancies and policies. It has practices in welcoming freshmen, honor codes, founders' days, homecomings, chapel services, honorary organizations, an "absence system," a requirement for "majoring," various learning "tracks" (exemption examinations, tutorial work, "scholars" programs, honors work), and other features of a complex organizational life. These factors, present to a greater or lesser degree in every college, comprise hurdles which the student must manage successfully in order both to remain on the campus and to secure its greatest blessing, a college degree.

Second, the college student must develop skill in the self-management of his responsibilities and opportunities in relation to the college's system of education. At times he will get pleasure out of learning for its own sake. The satisfaction of intellectual curiosity can be exciting and self-rewarding. Those students who are highly motivated to learn on their own and for themselves will enjoy their intellectual activities even when they do not fully see a connection between their present study and their future goals. They will appreciate, in Abraham Flexner's phrase, "the usefulness of useless knowledge." Flexner intended to point out the fact that one scarcely can distinguish in the long run between the various degrees of practical knowledge. What one person may assume to be utterly impractical may be for another, or for society in general, the most practical. After all, the practical may be simply the way we tend to characterize our own preferences. In life, the practical and the impractical (if that is the way the contrast should be stated) often are blurred in actual circumstances. Witness the development of the United States space program or the achievement of computerized information! What one learns at any time may seem to be of little immediate concern to anyone, including the learner, but in today's rapidly changing society all knowledge is precious and needful. Again, in an era of increasing leisure, stable and deep satisfactions come to individuals who maintain continuous and wide-ranging intellectual curiosity beyond the immediate and perhaps transitory requirements of living.

THE MANY-FACETED COLLEGE LIFE

But all college learning for most students will not be of that character. A large part of the learning undertaken will be in relation to college requirements, the competition of nonintellectual pursuits, the routinization of education (sometimes leading to discontent with courses, teaching, credits), and the ability of the student to organize his time and talents to be an academic success on terms that are established by others, mainly the faculty.

Intellectual activities, however, comprise only a part of the college experience. Social and personal experiences beyond the classroom, library, and laboratory constitute another significant component of college life. Some colleges merely "tolerate" this aspect of their students' activities, believing that the cocurriculum is a necessary but auxiliary and even intellectually debilitating feature of going to college. Other colleges tend to view the curriculum and the cocurriculum as engines traveling on parallel tracks. Each has its place, but each is separated from the other by an impassable gap. Still other colleges seek to minimize the differences between the curriculum and the cocurriculum, knowing that in the history of American higher education there has been easy passage from one sphere to the other, and believing that the life of the student outside of the formal and often required activities of the college constitutes one of the most fertile learning fields available to the college.

The policy of a college, whether announced or not, probably will have its influence upon the attitude and activities of its students. The late Harvard philosopher and mathematician, Alfred North Whitehead, gave credence to the educational value of social and personal experiences by saying: "The success of language in conveying information is vastly overrated, especially in learned circles . . . ; nothing can imply the defect of first hand experience."

But whether a college is organized to maximize the value of "first hand experience" or not, it will be had by the students. In fact, several surveys of students' interests in college indicate that students value the out-of-the-classroom experience even more than that of the classroom. A number of students find that their social and personal experiences are more crucial to them in the formation of their settled and mature values than anything they have experienced in the curriculum.

CAMPUS LIFE OUTSIDE THE CLASSROOM

The perceptive or sensitive student faces many problems or stresses in making his way in the life of the college outside of the classroom. The successful college student is an appropriately organized, self-managing individual who is able to effect a proper balance between the many demands which are made upon him for his interests, capacities, and time. He is able to establish a workable and satisfying compromise to the demands of the academic program and his desire to develop leadership, special skills, and friendships outside the classroom.

Life outside the classroom consists of engaging in informal and organized activities. The students spend a considerable amount of time in informal activities, such as those centered in dormitories, fraternity and sorority houses, student unions, and recreational facilities. Informal activities are based upon acquaintanceships and friendships already established, but they generally lead to the strengthening and enhancing of interpersonal relationships which reach a deeper level.

Organized activities, on the other hand, present numerous opportunities for most students. These are organized by students and "chartered" by the college. Commonly they are based upon the intellectual, social, athletic, religious, or other concerns of students. They provide opportunities to "learn by doing" (keeping minutes, presiding at meetings, arranging for a dance). They also provide a human-relations field in which students are able to test their interests and capacities to relate to others. Such experiences enable students to test their own views and values and to learn, even from negative situations, about the way in which small groups operate and seek to achieve their goals.

Induction into a fraternity or sorority may constitute a constructive experience for the student. These groups offer membership by invitation only and the resulting "rushing" procedures put considerable strain upon everyone involved. Obviously not all students are suited to fraternal groups. Intelligent decisions regarding membership commonly are based upon personality, financial cost, interest in the "fraternity way of life," previous patterns of living, and the student's careful weighing of the advantages and disadvantages of membership. In a later chapter, Dean Havice will discuss the long-established fraternity system and its potentials for the student.

Colleges also offer opportunities for students with special interests and talents to participate in student-government organizations and student publications.

Although every college is characterized by an all-college culture or set of experiences for its members, it is in one of the subcultures of the college that the student must seek his deepest satisfactions. Married students—who are in ever-increasing numbers—have their own way of life. The Ivy League or "Greek" subculture has its own pattern. The "independents" (sometimes highly organized and vocal) follow their own values. Even the self-defined social outcasts (they used to be called "beatniks") have their own subculture, replete with visual identifications, specialized activities, and core values. No student can accommodate himself to all of the subcultures of the campus. The successful college student will seek to operate within the one with which he is most congenial and to modify his adherence only in the light of personal crises or gradual changes in outlook.

College students also take part in a teenage fad culture by which they seek to satisfy their need for security and new experience. A strong, culturally supported feature of collegiate life is the desire to own or have available an automobile. The possession of an automobile (perhaps especially an "MGB" or a "TR4") is a campus badge of prestige and a ready source of pleasure. The college student who centers too much of his energies upon owning an automobile, however, may well find that his academic performance will suffer. Studies show that ownership of an automobile and the attainment of high grades have an inverse relationship to each other. A California junior college official stated: "I feel so sad sometimes when a student comes in to say he's withdrawing. Then I find out it's because the kid can't make the payments on his car."

College students also have particular though changing tastes in movies, literature, television, and "pop culture." Movies, novels, and television shows have a way of upcropping in popularity on local campuses and of spreading through the colleges of the land with surprising regularity. These interests cause some students to be innovators of trends, while others do their best to pay conformist allegiance to the current fads. Always changing, yet seemingly never changing, teenage culture on the college campus provides a significant set of experiences whereby the college student channels his interests and energies.

FOUR TYPES OF UNREST ON THE CAMPUS

The current generation of college students is characterized by unrest or activism. The activism is characterized more by spontaneous dynamics than by any one content or goal. Student complacency has been challenged, and the day of widespread student protests is here.

At least four types of student protests can be identified. First, some students have been engaged both on and off the campus in civil rights activities.

Second, a renewed interest in political affairs (including all levels of government, particularly international affairs) has led to the development of a long roster of political organizations, both left wing and right wing. Among the left groups are the Progressive Labor Clubs, Young Peoples Social League (right wing Socialist), the May 2nd Movement (anti-War in Vietnam), the small W.E.B. DuBois Clubs (Marxist), Youth Socialist Alliance (Trotskyite), and the Students for a Democratic Society (a liberal-radical socialist coalition), which is the largest leftist student organization with 2,000 members on 60 campuses.

The right wing is not without its student organizations, including the Young Americans for Freedom (claiming some 15,000 students), numerous unaffiliated conservative and individualist clubs, and a growing number of Ayn Rand societies.

Student groups of both the political left and the right are engaged not only in activities off the campus and in the community, but often with the deep involvement of professors, in campus oriented "sit-ins," "think-ins," all-night sessions on political issues, mass meetings, small study groups, and letter writing to campus newspapers.

Third, educational reform is another function of the student pro-
testers. The majority of America's students now attend "multiver-
sities" (large, conglomerate institutions). Some of these feature a
high degree of impersonal relations, both among students and
between faculty and students. Classes tend to be large and taught by
graduate assistants. Teaching is dull and routine—often without
reference to students' individual interests. The IBM card, say the
students, reigns in the multiversity. The four day National Conference on Student Stress, held in the fall of 1965 under the sponsorship
of the United States National Student Association with grants from
the National Institute of Mental Health and the Danforth Foundation, scored the ivory tower view of higher education. The Conference concluded that the American college student is far more
troubled about whether his education is relevant to the "outside
world" than he is by problems of sex, Vietnam, drugs, or the atomic
bomb. The revolt against irrelevancy and routine in higher education, sometimes resulting from tenured appointments and uninspired
professors, extends to more than a few campuses.

Fourth, students have been active in protesting social restrictions
upon their individual behavior. The notion, long held by educators
and by the law as well, that colleges have the responsibilities of
parents (*in loco parentis*) in regard to the private lives of students,
has formed the basis of many campus eruptions. Thus, in its editorial
response to the charge by one of the deans of Harvard College that
a "growing number of students" were taking dormitory visiting privileges as a "license to use the College rooms for wild parties or sexual
intercourse,[1] the *Crimson*, Harvard's undergraduate newspaper, held
that sexual freedom is analogous to freedom of religion and speech,
i.e., a matter of individuality or of private standards of conduct.[2]
The newspaper was affirming the individual as the ultimate measure
of the moral life. Curfew, off-campus excursions, beer drinking, and
other practices have been at the vortex of a swirling sea of controversy regarding the "rights" of college students.

Key words among the four types of student protests are "action"
and "personal commitment." Action there is aplenty, but the objective reference of "personal commitment" is not at all clear. Surely

---

[1] "Parietal Rules," *Harvard Crimson*, Vol. 141, No. 104, October, 1963.
[2] "Munro Voices Concern Over Parietal Use," *Harvard Crimson*, Vol. 141, No. 100,
September 26, 1963.

the commitment of the current generation of college activists is not for the ideologies of the past, including Marxism, although existentialist leaders of thought such as Albert Camus get their fair share of attention. Actually the stress is upon issues, not philosophies, and no systematic philosophical or political theory, either of the left or the right, holds the "personal commitment" of most of those mobilized for protests.

The period forecast by Professor Daniel Bell in his *End of Ideology* appears to be upon some college students. Finding no basis for accepting a transcendental metaphysics and having rejected all ideologies (including nationalism, Freudianism, etc.) as intellectually pretentious and indefensible, a minority of agitated students turn now to action, pure action: shades of Sorel and Gentile! Opportunistic, strangely passionate and even pragmatically altruistic, these college students today take delight in the fervor and stimulation of socially critical action itself.

YET MOST STUDENTS ARE CONFORMISTS

The bulk of college students, however, are not rebels; they are conformists. Perhaps only about 5% (possibly as many as 15%) of college students are in the ranks of the student protest movements. The others, the predominant majority, are quite content with things as they are, either within the college or within society at large. They may at times question anything and everything that occurs, but they do not permit themselves readily to break the bonds of campus and community acceptance. Despite their quiet distrust of established norms, they tend to look upon a college education as a passport into the land in which they see themselves in an affluent corner of The Great Society. One woman student projected her future in terms of wide-screen, living color: "I'll be happily married, with three kids. I'll be living on Long Island or in some suburb." A male student sees himself in the future as "worrying about the responsibilities of my job, my family, money, prestige, social standing."

The conformist pattern which characterizes the bulk of college students should not be viewed with surprise or disbelief by either college students or their elders. The conformist pattern is the dominant social expectancy in American society (as well as any society) and one which commonly is enforced by the several social institutions, including home, church, and school. Professor Edgar V. Friedenberg, for example, reports in *Coming of Age in America* on the findings of a research project in several typical high schools across the country. The project involved a series of hypothetical "problem" stories for which each student was asked to rate and discuss various given solutions. The stories and solutions were designed to show the the personal and social values each student rates most highly in himself and others.

The findings are unsurprising. The qualities consistently approved are well-roundedness, sociability and poise, "getting along," and adaptability. On the other hand, the attributes deemed to be least desirable are individuality, originality, personal commitment, and privacy.

Professor Friedenberg claims that the school systems often tend to stifle the very initiative and sense of personal autonomy that they should develop, whereby the values under which students live are recognized and changed for the better. He also concludes that those who assert their individuality are usually unprepared to do so in a constructive fashion; they are the "junkies" and delinquents, the jobless dropouts, and those who suffer from severe personal stress.

IDEALISM IS STILL A CAMPUS NORM

Certainly the current college generation is as "idealistic" as any in the past. As John Hersey's school principal says in *The Child Buyer*: "Sure there's a lot of leeway in the ideals of the younger generation, but I'll stake my career on the fact that idealism is on a higher plane among school kids than it is among their parents." Despite ambiguities and tensions arising from both social activism and social conformity, many college students have not only been able to order their lives in exemplary ways, contributing to their own private welfare, but they have been capable of contributions, both on and off the campus, that have sought to right injustices and have made telling contributions to the welfare of the ill, the poor, or the otherwise underprivileged, at hand and afar. This generation of college students also knows and prizes the high value of service. Increasingly, college students are coming to see that their adventuring towards social maturity can also be secured through sacrificial activities which are aimed at increasing the welfare of the less fortunate.

In dramatic and undramatic ways the students of the nation's colleges have been among those at the forefront of the recent efforts to claim full justice for all the people. In these and other ways college students have demonstrated that they are capable of self-management and, indeed, of living beyond themselves.

By adventuring in social maturity students are seeking to fulfill not only themselves as human beings but the basic principles of a college education. Nevitt Sanford, editor of *The American College*, has aptly summarized the college's responsibilities and the students' opportunities in the following way:

. . . If after four years the college turns out students who are broad and open to the world, have deep interests, and values that reflect their own criticism and best thought, who are sharp and flexible in their thinking and at the same time imaginative, curious, and capable of self-expression, and who now have good taste and are sensitive and discriminating with respect to the meaningful aspects of our culture, then this college is successful as an institution of learning . . . (such colleges) may be said to have furthered the development of their students as total personalities.[3]

[3] Nevitt Sanford, "Measuring the Success of a College," *Research Related to College Admissions* (Atlanta: Southern Regional Educational Board, 1963), p. 199.

4 / Richard F. Hettlinger

PORTRAIT OF THE FRESHMAN
AS A SEXUAL BEING

One volume in a recent series of books on sex education[1] carries the title *Life Can Be Sexual*, but it should run *Life Must Be Sexual*. For, despite the common phrase, sex is not something you do or something you have at one time or another, or even "The Most Satisfying Game Ever Invented,"[2] it is something you *are*. Whatever valid modifications and criticisms of Freud's views of anthropology, religion, and psychology have been made by his critics and successors, we can no longer pretend that sex is merely an external appendage to human nature, that man is "really" pure intellect, or that he is intended to live a "spiritual" life without bodily passions. Earl H. Brill's obituary notice *Sex is Dead and Other Postmortems*[3] is clever but premature, and the announcement by a sociologist, Dr. Sylvia Herz, that sex has been replaced by drugs as a subject of interest on campus[4] is hardly the equivalent of demonstration that students have suddenly become asexual. Whether we are sexually

---

[1] St. Louis, 1967.

[2] From an advertisement for *Advice from a Failure*, by Jo Coudert.

[3] New York, 1967.

[4] The conclusion, based on interviews with 150 students, was reported in *The New York Times*, November 27, 1967.

mature or immature, heterosexual or homosexual, playboys or priests, nymphomaniacs or nuns, spinsters or parents—we are and shall remain sexual so long as we are human beings. Whatever new dimensions pot and acid may bring to sexuality (and the early claims that marijuana and LSD are *direct* stimulants of sexual desire or pleasure, have now been retracted), students in the forseeable future will be consciously or unconsciously seeking to clarify and fulfill their roles as sexual beings. Indeed, one of the reasons why every new generation finds itself in conflict with its elders is that in the process of establishing self-identity each adolescent needs to achieve individuality *as a boy or a girl* and not as a hermaphrodite. Inevitably, therefore, the questioning (though not necessarily the abandonment) of parental sexual standards represents a normal and healthy aspect of growth into maturity. Dr. Morton S. Eisenberg has written that "The dissolution of the internalized model of the parents includes as well a partial negation of the values and standards of the parents that have been appropriate to childhood and have served well prior to this time. The temporary negation and realignment of these values is a necessary concomitant to growing up, and to the achievement of an independent and autonomous value system of one's own."[5] The rejection of parental sexual standards may not take an extreme form, and it often coexists with a continued respect for and partial dependence upon one's parents; but in order to move from adolescence to adulthood it is necessary eventually to test fears, ideals, and self-expectations in relationships with members of the other sex.

THE BACKGROUND OF THE PORTRAIT

Unfortunately, the task of achieving sexual maturity and self-identity is greatly complicated by the fact that in this area of life the practice and expectations of adults are exceptionally confusing. While there are few moral values to which our society gives uniform support, it does offer the adolescent in most areas some clear-cut standards to which he can respond either by acceptance, rejection, or qualification. For example, while there are thieves in every level of society, and from time to time executives of major corporations are sent to jail for dishonesty, there is virtual agreement as to the un-

[5] In *Sex Education and the New Morality*, The Child Study Association of America, New York, 1967, p. 13.

desirability of such practices and those convicted of embezzling funds are clearly condemned by society as a whole. In sexual matters, however, while our society has many rigorous laws governing even private sexual activity between adults, adolescents are presented with no consistent example by their elders. On the one hand young people are assured that sex is a matter of high moral concern, a sacred trust to be preserved for marriage; on the other hand the adult world without embarrassment engages in widespread sexual license and expands its multimillion dollar sales of everything from hair cream to foot lotion by trading on the sexual instincts of teenagers. Many American families recently received an unsolicited free sample of a "New Secret Weapon." The company concerned, having apparently given up the attempt to compete with toothpastes that reduce cavities, offered closeups of a young couple with the promise that their new product "gives your mouth sex appeal" by brightening the teeth, making your smile more appealing, keeping your whole mouth "crazy clean" and making you "nicer to look at, to talk to, to kiss."

Adolescent sexual development is made more difficult by the fact that (often with parental encouragement) expressions of sexual intimacy such as kissing, necking and petting are freely utilized in the formal and impersonal activities of the early teens. When a couple eventually discovers a relationship of greater depth and seriousness, they are in the position of having no way to express their love except that of going to bed together, and at this apparently arbitrary point parents declare an embargo! The young man of 18 or 19 is at the height of his sexual capacity and yet is officially denied, either by religious sanction, social convention or legal prohibition, any release of sexual energy other than "wet dreams." Since marriage, which is the only acceptable social solution to his problem, is frequently impracticable for the college student, he is subject to an almost intolerable tension for the years between his biological sexual peak and the time when he graduates.

The background of the portrait is even further confused by the disastrous failure of communication between the generations on the subject of sex. Despite some improvements, sex education both in the home and in the school remain largely ineffective, and while it has advanced from a discussion of the biology of the birds and bees to the provision of information about the reproductive organs of the human species, it still commonly makes no attempt to face the fundamental emotional and psychological problems. Midge Decter, in an article in *Harper's Magazine* acknowledged quite frankly that she had failed to give any advice to her daughters on the question whether they should engage in sexual relations with a man before marriage because she did not know how to answer such a question. She went on to explain that her uncertainty did not take the simple form of admitted ignorance, but rather found expression in a series of confident but contradictory statements on one side or the other, depending upon the circumstances. The confusion, and indeed cruelty, which resulted was, she suggested, representative of the defense of her entire generation against the implications of its own earlier sexual liberation. "If you begin as we all did with the proposition that lust is not only natural but life-giving and good, and if you travel the path from there straight and true, you arrive at complete sexual promiscuity. Lust as an independent value divorces itself from institutions, personal relations, and travels with utter unconcern from creature contact to creature contact. This is exactly how the Puritans understood the matter, and they were right. We understand it, too, in the pits of our stomachs if not in our minds, and scurry about to improvise our excuses. We do not want to be promiscuous, for if lust is simple, the other major human passions—vanity, pride, acquisitiveness—are not. . . . And if we do not want promiscuity for ourselves, we will certainly never be able to bear it in our children."[6] The readers of this book are the unfortunate heirs to this embarrassed confusion, and in most cases their parents have not even been successful in identifying and facing up to the nature of the problem, let alone offering any meaningful and realistic criteria by which to guide their personal sexual behavior.

A POPULAR CARICATURE

It is all too common for educators, clergy, judges, politicians, and journalists to point to the supposed debauchery and promiscuity of the student generation (whether it be evidenced by sexual activity, the wearing of long hair, or the use of psychedelic drugs) in order to distract attention from the adult failures to come to grips adequately with the problems raised by the sexual freedom that they

[6] "Sex, My Daughters and Me," *Harper's Magazine*, August 1967.

largely introduced. They readily forget that Kinsey found that the real breakdown of the Victorian sexual standards came with the generation born between 1900 and 1910, who were in college following the first World War. In the light of this it is appropriate to note the comment of Dr. Edward D. Eddy, President of Chatham College, that "The exposé (of student degeneration) is so persistent that one begins to wonder whether it is youth that is deteriorating or whether we are being treated to a purging of the guilt-ridden adult conscience."[7]

There are, however, some reasons for this caricature, inaccurate and unfair as it is. In the first place, today's students are not prepared, as their parents and grandparents were, to approve publicly one set of moral standards while practicing another. If honesty and integrity are counted virtues, I believe that today's students are among the most responsible of any age. In the second place, heavy petting, particularly in semipublic places, is a relatively recent development, and since both the older and the less educated members of society regard this as perverse, they tend to attribute to students a special degree of sexual debauchery. The use of petting, however, as a means of achieving intimacy and sexual release without intercourse often represents a moral choice—particularly for the girl. Third, students are much more able than their less educated peers to tell a good tale to the kids back home about the wild orgies that supposedly go on at college, and in many cases their reputation is more lurid than the facts warrant. The widespread use of *Playboy* foldouts for decorative purposes is frequently assumed to encourage slavering sensuality on the part of male students, whereas I suspect the motive is primarily revolt against the view of sex as dirty which students attribute to their elders. The fact that many fathers surreptitiously read *Playboy* but deny the same privilege to their sons only serves to strengthen this impression.

Finally, the concern of this generation with the present rather than the future and their preference for existential and situational ethics rather than for moral absolutes contributes to the caricature of young people as irresponsible and promiscuous. One of my students wrote as follows at the conclusion of a paper on Martin Buber: "My generation is a generation which realizes that one does not need to reach old age in order to know reality. We realize that life is not lived as a series of progressive precepts which leads eventually to the

[7] "What about the 'Sinful' Student," *Saturday Review*, March 19, 1966.

door of All-Knowing, or Truth, or Ultimate Reality. One will likely die well before he adequately "prepares" himself for such an ascension towards truth. My generation has realized that life is as real in this day as it will be in another fifty years. We have discovered that all of the world around us offers reality—that real time *is* now. Real time is encountered in our lives every day. Life *is* the concrete, the vivid, and the personal. Life *is* surfing, talking in the dark corners of a coffeehouse, miniskirts, movies, and dancing. Life is all of this. . . . We live life with our whole selves—passionately, actively—determined to live in real time, and not simply exist in preparation for real time." The interesting thing about this *credo* is that its author was as far as anyone can imagine from embodying the adolescent irresponsibility with which many adults associate such sentiments. He was typical of today's generation, but like most of you he was entirely different from the caricature which many older people prefer to draw.

In the circumstances it is not surprising that your generation has replied in kind. Just as one wit remarked that when God made man in his own image, man retaliated by making God in man's image, so it is widely assumed by those under thirty that sex is no fun at all beyond that dismal milestone, and that you'd best get all of it you can before your capacity for enjoyment is exhausted. I am glad to be able to report that this is no less a caricature than the distorted portrait of the young discussed above. A recent study of married college graduates found that twenty-nine percent of the men and thirty-five percent of the women reported more satisfying sexual experience in the later years of marriage than in the earlier years. Only twenty-four percent of the men and eighteen percent of the women affirmed the contrary, and the remainder had found sex no less satisfying with increasing age.[8]

THE FACTS ABOUT THE SUBJECT

My own conviction is that most of today's students are indeed dissatisfied with and unconvinced by the threats and moral absolutes which parents, clergy and teachers have handed out to them. But I also believe that students are not simply engaged in a blind rejection of moral values. They are looking for a more honest and rational approach to sex which will help them to make sense of it. They are

[8] Elmer Roper poll reported in the *Saturday Evening Post*, December 31, 1966.

disillusioned by the hypocrisy of the society in which they have grown up; but they are not irresponsible, perverse, or promiscuous. They sense the mystery and dangers of sex as well as its delights. They want to develop satisfying personal relationships. They are at times possessed by an exhilarating, threatening, overwhelming need to express their sexuality. Yet they are confronted by prohibitions and taboos which attempt, however unsuccessfully, to prevent that expression. They are confused (even if they prefer not to acknowledge it) rather than degenerate; the victim of society's dishonesty rather than a proper scapegoat for its justification. Above all they are ready to listen if anyone will lift the veil of bigotry and prudery from the subject and help them appreciate the depths and beauty of sexual relationships. However much it may be true that we live in "The Permissive Society" in which "Anything Goes"[9] most students are not selfish users of other people for mere physical satisfaction or adherents of the philosophy of egotistical hedonism advocated by Dr. Albert Ellis in *Sex and the Single Man*.[10]

Of course, a good deal of thoughtless and purely sensual sexual activity goes on at every college or university, and some male readers may enjoy a certain bravado in being a member of a group so notorious for its supposed virility. But there is little basis in fact for the portrait of the freshman as a young rake. Kinsey found twenty years ago that the percentage of males of college-level education who engaged in sexual intercourse between the ages of 16 and 25 was about one-third *lower* than the figure for their less educated contemporaries. A recent study of 3,000 undergraduates on campuses in California concluded that "Our investigations do not confirm the popular stereotype of widespread sexual promiscuity. . . . Sexual intimacy, where it occurs, takes place in the context of a relationship that is serious rather than casual."[11] Gael Greene in her valuable study *Sex and the College Girl* wrote that although many a girl in this "orgasm-oriented decade" talks loudly about "the unquenchable fire of her female hormones,"[12] she is more likely to be looking for affection and love. Dr. Seymour Halleck of the University of Wisconsin believes that promiscuity is generally symptomatic of alienated students

[9] The cover story for *Newsweek*, November 13, 1967.   [10] New York, 1963.
[11] The study was conducted by Dr. Joseph Katz, and a team of 18 psychologists and psychiatrists and will be published by Jossey-Bass under the title *Growth and Constraint in College Students*.
[12] New York, 1964, p. 95.

who are incapable of loving ideals or loving others.[13] Father Joseph Walsh, CSP, Catholic Chaplain at Brandeis University, in an article in *Commonweal* concluded that "After a careful reading (of several studies) . . . my own experience, and that of my fellow campus ministers, is confirmed: students approach sex as a moral matter, i.e., as an area of serious responsibility and concern. The image of large numbers of college students sleeping around, indiscriminately indulging in sex for kicks and pleasure without any concern for consequences or permanence appears to reflect more the frustrated yearnings of writers and readers than it does actual campus life."[14]

Relatively few students are promiscuous in the sense that they engage in heavy petting or intercourse with several partners in the course of casual encounters. The great majority will justify sexual intimacy on the highly moral ground that "love makes it right so long as nobody gets hurt." This is not the traditional sexual standard, and it is obviously open to abuse and convenient manipulation, but it cannot be dismissed as immoral or identified with "fornication." That term, so beloved of religious leaders with little imagination or understanding of history, is drawn from a cultural context in which sexual intimacies outside marriage could be assumed to be of a promiscuous type. The biblical writers who use the term take no account whatsoever of the kind of relationship which exists in the twentieth century between a couple who are dating or engaged. But those who affirm that love does make it right must be challenged to take their position seriously rather than dismissed as irresponsible.

SOME QUESTIONS FROM A VIEWER

Oscar Wilde's book, *The Portrait of Dorian Gray*, depicts a man whose debased and selfish life began to show its effects not on his own features but on a portrait painted in his youth, which was in his possession. He then set out to live the life of a Don Juan all the more effectively because he continued to present an appearance of naïve innocence to every girl whom he seduced. It was a melodramatic story and was later made into an equally melodramatic movie, but its relevance to our theme is obvious. The claim that "love makes it

---

[13] A paper read to the American Psychiatric Association, as reported in *The New York Times*, May 12, 1967.
[14] February 24, 1967, p. 590.

right" may be merely a cover for selfish satisfaction, a rationalization of irresponsible promiscuity, a way of persuading a boy or a girl to satisfy your personal desires. But if it is followed with real integrity the principle "love makes it right" will not be less but more demanding than the legalism it has replaced. Whoever guides his or her life by this high-sounding ideal must, for example, distinguish between love and lust, between love and infatuation, between love and the impersonal use of another human being for physical pleasure, aggression or security. "Love makes it right" is commonly taken to mean "love makes intercourse right." But the term "love" covers a wide range of relationships; and different kinds of sexual intimacy are made "right" by different degrees of love. If love is something more than urgent desire, it cannot be immediately assumed that the beginning of love is an adequate basis for every sexual act. You can hardly treat a boy or a girl whom you know only superficially as a real person. We consider a girl who generally goes to bed on a first date a tramp. There is some relationship between the self-knowledge and commitment of a boy and a girl to each other and the degree of sexual intimacy they can enjoy with integrity.

Personally I do not think that any external authority should attempt to determine at what stage in a growing relationship a couple can move appropriately from kissing to deep kissing, from petting to heavy petting, and from heavy petting to intercourse. But in many cases, I suspect that the type of relationship established in college does not really justify (in the sense of providing adequate emotional support for and integrity to) the final intimacy of intercourse. Yet in the context of the confused and contradictory pressures to which our society subjects its younger members, I believe there can be times when "love makes it right" in the full sense—when intercourse may be the appropriate way of expressing and preserving a deep and meaningful relationship. Love does occasionally reach a degree of maturity of which intercourse is the only appropriate expression, when economic and other factors make marriage impossible.

Nevertheless, I suggest that *ideally* the final intimacy of intercourse should be preserved until the time when a couple have accepted each other permanently and fully in marriage. Even engagement is temporary and tentative, and so-called "trial marriage" is a contradiction in terms because in this relationship the couple is trying each other out rather than committed to each other for better or worse. If a girl goes all the way with someone she does not eventually marry, how is she to express the unique involvement and intimacy of her sexual relationship to the man she does marry? The boy who goes to bed with a girl he does not marry may put her out of the market for the kind of marriage that many men think desirable: namely, marriage with a virgin or with a girl who has not been to bed with another man.

No couple can be sure that they will benefit if they engage in the ultimate intimacy of intercourse before the ultimate commitment of love in marriage. Dr. Lester Kirkendall in his study of *Premarital Intercourse and Interpersonal Relationships*[15] found that, in an appreciable number of cases, when an engaged couple had intercourse together it resulted in a weakening of their relationship, the breaking of the engagement, or a later decision to discontinue the practice until after marriage. To capitulate *prematurely* to the pressures of our double-faced society, to the expectation of your peer group, or to the joys of the sexual urge, may well be to the disadvantage of love in the long run. The man who argues that intercourse is the appropriate expression of love may in fact be seeking merely to bolster his own sense of inadequacy or to stifle some inner loneliness. He may be looking for a mother substitute or a status symbol. He may be using sex as an expression of aggressive power over another human being. The girl may be using her sexual attractiveness as a means of manipulating the boy to give her other things, or looking for a man to fill the gap left by an absent or withdrawn father. Three out of five of those in the *Seventeen* survey who had engaged in intercourse stressed inner insecurity, often resulting from lack of parental love, as a reason for their actions.[16] Finally, each has to recognize that he or she may be simply using the other to affirm independence from the square world represented by the college administration.

SOME UNOBSERVED NUANCES IN THE PORTRAIT

One of the reasons why we fail sometimes to treat another person as a full human being and not as an "It," and one of the reasons why one of the couple who are in love gets badly hurt is that students are largely ignorant of the differences between male and female sex-

[15] New York, 1966.   [16] July, 1967, p. 129.

uality. The portrait of the freshman as a sexual being is a composite one, and it is all too easily assumed that modern knowledge has demonstrated the essential sexual identity of the two very different subjects. For example, many men take it for granted that girls share their enthusiasm for intercourse as an expression of love. We tend to assume without question that any girl in her right senses will find our personal erotic attentions virtually irresistible. This very questionable androcentrism is further supported by a secondhand knowledge of recent research which is supposed to have established that a girl enjoys the same sexual activity as men do *and at the same stage in the relationship*. Any hesitation on her part is therefore quite sincerely assumed to be due to a hangover from Victorian inhibitions. Not infrequently a man says "She asked me to stop, but I knew she didn't mean it." But while Kinsey, and more recently, the Masters and Johnson report, *Human Sexual Response*,[17] have indeed made it clear that women are as capable as men of enjoying sexual orgasm and that the physiological experience is virtually identical, they do not justify the assumption that most girls are as ready or as eager for intercourse as an expression of love outside marriage during the teens or early twenties as are most men. Kinsey found that the peak of female orgasmic capacity and need came in the late twenties, about ten years later than it does among the male population. This may, of course, be largely a sociological phenomenon and there is some indication that the statistical difference is already somewhat narrowed, partly as a result of Kinsey's study. But it is still a fact, to which any man who claims to love a girl must surely give attention, that the more intimate kinds of genital sexuality, which for men represents a highly desirable experience from the middle teens on, are frequently of quite minor importance to many women until much later. Despite the title of their book (which I think should have been correctly called *Human Sexual Orgasm*), Masters and Johnson in other writings have very clearly affirmed that orgasm plays a markedly different role in the total sexual interests of the girl. Men who welcome the equality of women in sexual matters should surely allow their partner equal rights in deciding *when* she is ready to enjoy or accept the final intimacy of intercourse. Indeed, he has to ask himself the question whether a full respect for her feelings and her real needs may require him to say "Because

17 Boston, 1966.

I love her we won't." Certainly he will abstain from the petty black-mail implied in the challenge "If you loved me, you'd go to bed with me."

The problems of confusion and misunderstanding are not by any means on the male side alone. Because of the inaccurate public impression of the implications of Kinsey, and Masters and Johnson, there is a widespread tendency for girls to feel that they must, how-ever little they desire it, express their sexuality in intercourse. Partly because Kinsey started from the very male assumption that sex and orgasm are identical (and only a male would have talked about the six types of sexual *outlet*), it is widely supposed that if girls do not desire or enjoy orgasm the depth and reality of their sexuality is being called in question. Such a suggestion is, of course, as strongly resented as it is absurd. Recent studies have made it clear that while girls are no less sexual than men in their teens and early twenties, sexuality is for them something much more diffuse, less genital, person-oriented, and linked to the monthly menstrual cycle. Without necessarily wanting to have a child, a girl is therefore almost always consciously or subconsciously concerned in every act of sexual inter-course with the question of the security and happiness of a potential child. Indeed, there is reason to think that with all the available contraceptives on the market today, when one girl out of every five who has intercourse outside marriage becomes pregnant it is not merely accidental. As one psychiatrist has put it: "Although con-sciously they may believe that they have no desire to have a baby, unconsciously they may harbor a strong wish to prove themselves adequate as women by providing a child. This unconscious need for fulfillment is often manifested by a refusal to use contraception or by 'forgetfulness' in this regard."[18]

Because the girl's sexuality is in many ways less dramatic and intense, less urgently requiring orgasm and release, and more affected by the quality of the relationship she has with the boy, she is more able than he to abstain from intercourse without nervous tension or psychic frustration. When she suggests at an advanced stage of petting that she would rather play a record on the stereo, she is fre-quently unaware of the fact that she is asking something virtually

[18] Graham B. Blaine, Jr., Chief of Psychiatry, Harvard University Health Services, in the *New York State Journal of Medicine*, July 15, 1967, pp. 1969–1970.

impossible of the boy who has by this time reached a degree of sexual arousal which can only be satisfied in orgasm. Girls who complain that men don't know when to stop, or that allowing them one degree of intimacy leads inevitably to further advances, are displaying their ignorance of male sexuality and measuring the man's emotions and arousal by their own very different standards. Just as the man needs to ask himself whether, if he really loves a girl, he should abstain from pressing her to accept intercourse, the girl must equally ask herself whether, if she really loves the boy, she is being fair to him in breaking off intimacies when he is at the pitch of arousal which can only be satisfied by orgasm.

AN ANGRY REBUKE TO THE ARTIST

President Johnson caused a considerable furor early in 1967 when he rejected a portrait of himself by Peter Hurd, which had been commissioned by the White House Historical Association, as "the ugliest thing I ever saw." I suspect that some readers of this book are at the point of a similar reaction to the portrait I have sketched of the freshman as a sexual being. Are there aspects of adolescent sexuality which I have minimized and which, if ignored, are liable to result in impoverishment or disaster? For example, it is widely believed that unless a boy engages in sexual intercourse he is bound to suffer some loss of sexual capacity or power. As an advertisement for a recent movie put it, "There are hungers no man can deny." Kinsey pointed out twenty years ago that this is an old wives' tale entirely without foundation, and more recently the omniscient *Playboy Advisor* replied to an enquiry: "Abstinence, as such, is neither good nor bad for the health. What does affect the individual's well-being are the circumstances of, and the motivation for, his abstention. . . ; if the motivation for abstention is conscious and rational, no harm will be done. If, on the other hand, the motivation is based on guilt or fear, then strong conflicts, feelings of frustration and intense anxiety will ensue."[19] Thus, the man who abstains from sexual intimacy because of a basic fear of his own sexuality, or because of an oversensitive super-ego may be in need of therapy; but the man who abstains out of love and respect for a girl is in no way

[19] *Playboy*, November 1967, p. 61.

harming himself physically or psychologically and indeed is more likely to be demonstrating significant powers of maturity and strength.

There is a widespread impression that alternative means of sexual release, such as masturbation or petting to orgasm are physically or psychologically harmful. Masturbation, or any of the sexual behavior which runs contrary to the individual's conscience or religious conviction, can indeed be harmful; but "excessive masturbation" is a virtual impossibility, since the nervous response is exhausted long before repetition of the physical act can do any damage. Others are under the impression that premarital petting to orgasm is liable to make sexual intercourse more difficult to achieve in marriage. However, Kinsey found that women are much more likely to have difficulty in adjusting to intercourse after marriage if they have had intercourse without orgasm before marriage, than if they have engaged in mutual petting, which apparently bears no relation to marital sexual problems.

Many believe that there is a correlation between premarital sexual intercourse and successful marriage, but once again this is not justified by any available factual information. The idea that differences in the size of male and female genitals can lead to permanent problems in intercourse, and that premarital experimentation is important in order to discover whether a couple are physically compatible is entirely fallacious. Despite frequent assertions to the contrary, Kinsey never suggested that premarital intercourse bore any relation to successful and happy marriage, and other authorities using Kinsey's data or independent research have concluded that on the whole a husband and wife without experience of premarital intercourse have a higher chance of marital success. The fact of the matter is that there are not available any scientific or statistical facts which will relieve us of the responsibility for decisions in this area. There are some for whom premarital intercourse is a means of sustaining and strengthening a relationship of love, and there are some for whom it is (even if undertaken with integrity) harmful and disadvantageous. None of us knows with any certainty what the consequences for us will be. All we can do is to acquaint ourselves as fully as possible with the facts, to examine our motives as objectively as possible, to be entirely honest and open with each other, and to recognize the dangers to which sexual activity lays us open because of its inseparable connection with the very foundations of our personality.

PORTRAIT OF THE STUDENT AS A MATURE SEXUAL BEING

Photographs taken at high school for the freshman handbook are already out of date by the time the boy or girl arrives on campus, as any upperclassman or faculty member trying to identify newcomers from this source knows only too well. The portrait for the sorority or fraternity pledge class is unrecognizable when it is time to sit for the graduation picture. Likewise, the portrait of the freshman as a sexual being will be out of date when he or she becomes a sophomore, a senior, or an alumnus. For college is a place to mature sexually. These are years in which a student has an unequaled opportunity to develop as a personal being—as a sexual being—without the cloying restraints of close family supervision and the assumption by friends and neighbors that he will continue to conform to the patterns of behavior which he (and they) have established in childhood and adolescence. College represents for him the move from the town culture (to use Harvey Cox's phrase in *The Secular City*)[20] to the relative anonymity of the academic equivalent of technopolis. The freshman can be himself—he can make himself—in the next four years. He should not be one of the eighty-five percent who merely fit in and conform: he should rock the boat a little and keep it moving, open what *Esquire* magazine has taught us to call synapses,[21] hold fast to that state of mind which is youth—freedom from the past, openness to the future, questioning of the establishment, rejection of merely conventional rules.

He should remember, however, that though he is inevitably moving towards adulthood, he has not yet attained it, and many different portraits may be possible before he can be recognized as a mature sexual being—indeed it is doubtful if any of us quite deserves that description. The process of developing independence and sexual identity will inevitably bring him into conflict at times with the regulations inseparable from any institution, and all too often these will be restrictive, old-fashioned, arbitrary and ridiculous in their

20 New York, 1965.
21 "The Publisher's Page," September 1967. I am indebted to this "Annual Attempt to Bridge The Generation Gap" for several phrases in this paragraph.

attempts to control his private life. Some colleges and universities now accept the suggestion of the Group for the Advancement of Psychiatry that "sexual activity privately practiced with appropriate attention to the sensitivities of other people should not be the direct concern of the administration."[22] But even in the most enlightened and sympathetic academic community the point at which private acts take on public implications is differently estimated by students, faculty, and administration.

In the circumstances it may well appear to be a matter of honor and pride to knock the official standards and to "show adults you are going to do exactly what you want to do, regardless of what they think."[23] But remember that college life, with its abnormal tendency towards the isolation of a narrow age group, its lack of opportunities to retreat from the pressures of dormitory life, its enforced confrontation with members of the other sex (or its enforced separation from them on all-male or all-female campuses) may make demands on you that are inconsistent with your personal growth. For freedom is not primarily the opportunity to act in ways denied you in the past, to experiment with sexual behavior previously forbidden or unavailable. True freedom, to use a definition that goes back to Plato, is freedom to be yourself, to develop your peculiar character and potentialities.

The possibility for such development depends on new freedoms of choice at college—freedom from a carefully controlled academic program, freedom to stay away from church or synagogue, freedom to study through the night and sleep through the day, freedom to get drunk even if you find it unpleasant, and freedom to go to bed with a boy or girl you love if you choose. Identity with the peer group in tension with the adult world is an important element in the achievement of that self-identity, that final cutting of the umbilical cord, of which we spoke at the beginning of this chapter. Freedom in its fullest sense will not be achieved by rebellion for the sake of non-conformity by the man who has intercourse with the first girl he can *because* the Dean says it's forbidden or by the girl who is promiscuous to *spite* her parents.

The greatest threat to your freedom and growth as a sexual being

[22] *Sex and the College Student* (New York, 1966), p. 126.
[23] Quoted by a West Virginia University journalist as a frequent reason for premarital intercourse in the LOOK Magazine publication *Youth Quake*, 1967, p. 10.

may not be the restrictions imposed by the school authorities but the pressures and expectations of your peers. It may be more difficult to resist the demands (usually of a vocal but persuasive minority) that you prove your virility in a "gang bang" than to control your own sexual urge. It may be more difficult to refuse to join the non-virgin club than to persuade your date to be satisfied with petting. But the man who is captive to the obligation to reject everything his parents have stood for is no more free than the man who is captive to the obligation to accept their dictates. The girl who meekly submits to the student code against her better judgment is no more mature than the girl who meekly submits to the Dean's decrees as to what is morally right. Freedom is the capacity to maintain the protest of youth against rules for rules' sake and the readiness to benefit from the experience and insights of maturity. Adulthood is not achieved automatically when the freshman photograph is out of date: it is attained if the graduation portrait reflects independence, integrity, and sexuality capable of the deepest personal relationship of love.

DRINK AND DRUGS ON THE CAMPUS

At 10:15 on a morning early in 1963, Mr. Harry Asher, a physiologist at the University of Birmingham, England, went on a "trip." He went on his "trip" by taking 30 millionths of a gram of LSD, a powerful hallucinogenic drug. He was, on that morning, a subject in a carefully controlled scientific experiment. His actions were observed and directed by professional researchers at all times. Let's accompany Mr. Asher on his "trip":

The early experiences were wholly delightful. There was a feeling of exhilaration and self-confidence such as is rarely experienced, and an exaggerated tendency to laugh at anything at all. The failure of anyone else to understand what the joke was became in itself irrepressibly funny. The laughter became difficult to control. Things got funnier and funnier, and I laughed until I was in a condition of painful spasm with tears running down my cheeks.

Then the visual distortions began. I noticed a patch of sunlight on the floor. Because its brightness appeared to be fluctuating I inquired if clouds were crossing the sky. No, the light was really steady. . . .

At about this time, distortions of depth also began to occur. The object that made the greatest impression on me was a pair of spectacles worn by one of the assistants. They stood out in front of his face, which itself was increased in depth. . . .

At their height, the depth distortions alternated. At one moment the feet would seem to be far away and small. . . . Then the effect would reverse and the legs and body would look very short. The feet appeared to be about eighteen inches below my eyes, and it seemed that they had come up rather than that I had gone down.[1]

This experience of Mr. Asher is similar to the reaction of a college student who, under the influence of LSD, spent twenty-four frightened hours convinced he was only six inches tall.

The morning passed for Mr. Asher. Late in the afternoon he took a walk:

There were two of me walking down the corridor. The two people were not very accurately localized in space, but the main one corresponded in position to where I would have been had there been only one of me. The shadowy, or more tenuous individual, the naughty one, was slightly to the left. . . .

The main person was really me, but in an improved form. He was a very strong character. He had an effortless strength that I never knew before that I possessed. The other individual on the left was much less well known to me.

"Why not jump out of a window?" he said to me.

The invitation had a compulsive quality which was difficult to resist. But just as I was considering it, the main person answered for me, speaking with effortless strength.

"Of course not. Don't be such a bloody fool."[2]

Mr. Asher was driven home by a staff member and, after a long, confused and roundabout trip, answered his wife's invitation to enter the house.

"No thank you, darling. I think I won't come in just now. I will go for a walk. Keep the children away from me, will you please?"

I had a compulsive urge to do violence to my children and did not like to tell her about it.[3]

An hour and a half later, after numerous trips around the block, Mr. Asher returned to his home.

[1] Harry Asher, "They Split my Personality," *Saturday Review*, 46, June 1, 1963, p. 39
[2] *Ibid.*, p. 42.   [3] *Ibid.*

"Keep the children away from me please!" . . . I could not convey to her how important it was that she should do this, nor do I know myself to this day how great the gap was between the violent thoughts and their possible execution.[4]

Later that evening, rather than leave Mr. Asher home with the children, Mrs. Asher took him to dinner at the home of friends. After dinner he began a discourse on the subject of fireplaces and the theory of heating dwellings.

"There is a little man on the roof. . . . He has a thermometer in his hand. . . . He measures the temperature of the smoke. 'Bad,' he says. 'Too hot now.' With any convenient apparatus he measures the mass of smoke and hot air. . . ."

My host politely adjusted his features to simulate interest, but his distress was apparent.[5]

He left the dinner party and went home to the first of many sleepless nights. During the night he saw an eye very clearly in the darkness. Earlier, shortly after first swallowing the LSD, he saw teeth. Both are commonly seen.

Next day, unfortunately, I still was not right. There was no question of getting out of bed. I just lay there talking, babbling rather, mostly about my past. Often I cried, which was very distressing for my wife, who naturally thought it represented a condition of deep grief. As far as I can remember it did not. It was as though my body were crying and I was outside it. . . .[6]

Mr. Asher spent several days in bed, first babbling and crying, then apathetic and limp. His overwhelming fear during these days had to do with his loss of "will power."

The drug had paralyzed the "will power" section (of the mind). I can remember saying, "I'm prepared to do battle against ordinary affections: but hell!—I've nothing left to do battle *with*. This drug has cut me off at the source. It's completely knocked out the *will power*."

After a fortnight I was still very jumpy and susceptible to illusions. . . . One morning on looking into the sink, I saw this enormous creature standing at one edge. It looked so real that I frankly did not know what sort of action to take. Rather feebly I blew on it, and to my horror it

4 *Ibid.*   5 *Ibid.*, p. 42–43.   6 *Ibid.*, p. 43.

made grotesque movements, impossible for any normal insect to achieve; and with this movement it fluttered around the sink.[7]

As it turned out, the huge insect seen by Mr. Asher was a black, charred piece of paper. Yet the fear he experienced was real and overpowering. And this occurred two weeks after taking a bit of chemical so small that it could be seen only through a microscope.

Not all "trips" with LSD and other hallucinogenic drugs are as unhappy as this one of Mr. Asher. Many students report joy, elation, ecstasy, and freedom as a result of LSD or marijuana. As a matter of fact, one cannot depend on one's reaction to the drug; it is different for every person and, in many cases, with each experience.

DRUGS ON THE COLLEGE CAMPUS

In recent months the taking of drugs by college students has been a topic of great interest and concern, resulting in newspaper and magazine articles, urgent letters of warning from the government, roundtable discussions and lectures. I am sure that there is scarcely a college student left who has not heard or read about the use of drugs by college students. This chapter will attempt to focus, not so much upon the taking of the drugs, which is, after all, an individual decision, but upon the *effects* of using drugs.

The use of drugs is not new. Since the beginning of recorded history, man has attempted to escape from the unpleasantness of his environment. For centuries he has resorted to various habit-forming substances, such as coffee, tea, alcohol and tobacco. Once a person became a habitual user of these substances, then it was difficult to do without them.

Removing oneself from direct encounter with the world and its problems was seen to be important for the future Utopias as well. Huxley, in his novel, *Brave New World*, has the rulers of this world develop Soma, a drug which has "all the advantages of Christianity and alcohol, (and) none of their drawbacks." Soma becomes for the workers of the Brave New World—those who have to do the disagreeable chores—a short cut to happiness.

Some college students of today, as well as others, are looking for their own particular brand of Soma. Listen to the words of several of those who found it:

[7] *Ibid.*

Incident: "Man, I've been flying for three days on LSD. Did I kill my wife? Did I rape anybody? What have I done?" As it turned out, this 30-year-old medical student (third year, passing grades) *had* murdered his mother-in-law, a 57-year-old junior high school teacher, with a kitchen knife. As he was booked for murder he kept repeating: "I'm really high. I'm really high." He had taken LSD "just to experiment with its effects."[8]

Incident: One man under the drug suddenly began to stroke the air while listening to Beethoven's Fifth and exclaimed that every motif had a different texture: "That one is pure silk." "This is sharp, rough gravel," or, "Now I can feel an angel's gown." Others report that they can smell music, hear colors and touch the texture of odors.[9]

The blending of sense perceptions—hearing colors, smelling music, touching smells—is called synesthesia, and is a common experience under LSD.

Incident: "What I really discovered under LSD is love. Some call it God and I like this term, too. It is God, it is love. . . . God is love and therefore Love is God."[10]

Incident: Under LSD, colors become enormously rich and vivid. "One person, while being driven in a car, exclaimed at the red light of an ordinary traffic light: 'It is the most astonishingly glorious red in the whole world. It is *ultimate* red.' "[11]

Incident: An honor student at Amherst College burst into the home of a 74-year-old widow and ran shouting and screaming through the house. Finally he beat and choked her. As he was apprehended, he bit two policemen. Three weeks before his graduation he was expelled.

Incident: On Good Friday, twenty seminary students took pills—ten pills were a strong hallucinatory drug, ten were placebos or neutral substances. None of the students knew which was which. During the worship service that followed "every one of the first ten (the ones who took the drug) underwent an intense religious experience which had 'lasting' beneficial effects. These experiences ranged from transports of joy to a conviction of oneness with the entire world, a loss of sense of self and an intuition concerning the real truth of the universe."[12]

---

[8] "Murder by LSD?" *Newsweek*, 67:17, April 25, 1966, p. 29.
[9] Leonard Robinson, "Hearing Color, Smelling Music, Touching a Scent," *New York Times Magazine*, August 22, 1965, p. 50.
[10] *Ibid.*   [11] *Ibid.*   [12] *Ibid.*

Incident: A physician who took LSD reported the following: "I am coming to pieces at the seams. I am breaking open like a beautiful yellow, yellow orange! What delight. I have never had this kind of ecstasy! I am out of my own yellow, yellow orange skin at last—I am free!—I am Free! Freeeee!"[13]

Incident: An insurance salesman saw it somewhat differently: "Everything is shattering into bits. I am breaking up. Something awful is going to happen. Black! Black! Something horrible is going to happen. My mind is breaking up. My whole head is coming apart. This is hell. I am in hell. Get me out of this! Get me Out!"[14]

Incident: Aldous Huxley, writing about his experience with drugs, says: "Confronted by a chair which looked like the Last Judgment—or to be more accurate, by a Last Judgment which, after a long time and considerable difficulty, I recognized as a chair—I found myself all at once in a panic. This, I thought, was going too far, even though the going was into intense beauty and deeper significance."[15]

I could go on and on, reciting incident after incident; yet the message should be clear. The taking of drugs is a completely unpredictable and intense experience.

THE MATURE INDIVIDUAL

It is extremely difficult, if not impossible, to define adequately a mature person. Yet, in order to put the use of drugs on the campus into a meaningful perspective, it is worth a brief attempt.

The college student moves into an environment in which he is expected to assume more and more responsibility for his own actions. No one tells him when to get up, when to go to bed, and when to study. He is left to decide for himself whether or not he will attend class, whether or not he will read the assigned chapters.

Some college students are ready for this responsibility and accept it; others are not ready and they are threatened by it. They feel very uncomfortable and do not know why. A common human response to threat is escape, attempting to deny the existence of a problem by running away from it or refusing to admit that it exists.

It is my belief that the maturity of an individual college student lies, not in the act itself of accepting responsibility or refusing it, but in a willingness to accept the consequences of the action! In

---

[13] *Ibid.*   [14] *Ibid.*   [15] *Ibid.*

other words, under certain circumstances, one might be better off running away from a problem, or at least postponing its solution until another time. Perhaps one doesn't feel up to facing the problem physically or emotionally. Or perhaps more information will be available at a later date. *But he then should be willing to accept the consequences of his own action.* He should be willing to accept any negative (or positive) consequences which come to him as a result of his decision.

In the college setting, then, maturity is not measured so much by always attending classes, or always reading the assigned chapters. Perhaps something else comes up—a visiting lecturer, for example —and the student decides to attend the lecture rather than read the chapters. It may be that in the long run the educational experience of the lecture will be superior to reading the chapter. But the student must be willing to accept the consequences of his decision; he must be willing to accept the responsibility of not having read the chapter.

Thus the issue is *not* to get drunk or not to get drunk, it is *not* to smoke pot or not to smoke pot, *not* to take LSD or not to take LSD. The issue is in understanding the effects of these acts and accepting their consequences.

A problem arises, however, when maturity is defined in this way. In order to accept the consequences of any act, one must have knowledge regarding the possible outcomes. This chapter is not an attempt to stop anyone from getting drunk every weekend, from taking a "trip" with LSD, from getting "high" from smoking pot. It is planned to give information about the consequences of using drugs, which will allow students to make their own decisions regarding the use of them.

DRUGS COMMONLY USED BY COLLEGE STUDENTS

There are several categories of habit-forming and addicting drugs which are widely used. A rather complete chart, prepared by the Boston Police Department, appears on pages 58–59.

It is generally agreed that except on a very few campuses in urban areas, the narcotic drugs such as heroin and morphine are not used by college students. Young people who take these drugs never reach college.

There are few colleges, however, that have not seen a significant rise in the use of the new psychedlic or consciousness-expanding drugs such as LSD, as well as a rise in the use of marijuana. As Freedman and Powelson say, "On campuses where cosmopolitan students congregate—large city campuses or prestigious small liberal arts colleges —the proportion of students who experiment with pot or LSD may run as high as ten percent."[16] Others disagree. In a Senate hearing investigating the use of drugs on campus, a prominent senator indicated that based on evidence received from the medical directors of

Vice Control Unit—Boston Police Department

Chart of Habit-Forming and Addicting Drugs

DRUG	SOURCE	HOW TAKEN	EFFECT	CHARACTERISTICS
Opium (n)	Poppy	Smoked Chewed	Sleep Relieves pain	Depressant; withdrawal symptoms
Morphine (n)	Alkaloid of opium	Injection Orally	Pleasurable sensation Relieves pain	Depressant; same as opium
Heroin (n)	From morphine	Injection Sniffing Smoked	Euphoric	Depressant; 5 times as potent as morphine
Dilaudid (n)	From morphine	Injection	Sleep	Substitute for morphine—4 times as potent
Codeine (n)	From morphine	Injection Orally	Mild relief	Not as potent as morphine
Cocaine (n)	Coca leaf	Chewing Sniffing	False courage Delusions Nervousness	Intense stimulant; toxic; rare in U.S.; no withdrawal symptoms
Marijuana	Hemp (Cannabis) (Hashish)	Chewing Smoking Infusion In drinks	Variable Excitement Stupefaction	Unpredictable effects; will power destroyed; violent behavior; hallucinations. No physical dependence
Peyote	Cactus plant	Chewing Orally	Visual hallucinations of colors	Effect similar to cocaine

16 Mervin Freedman and Harvey Powelson, "Drugs on Campus: Turned On and Turned Out," *Nation*, 202:5, January 31, 1966, p. 25.

Vice Control Unit—Boston Police Department—*Continued*

Chart of Habit-Forming and Addicting Drugs

DRUG	SOURCE	HOW TAKEN	EFFECT	CHARACTERISTICS
Demerol (n) (Isonipecaine)	Synthetic	Injection	Analgesic Between morphine and codeine	Morphine-like character, same addicting effects. Habit-forming
Amphetamine (Benzedrine, Dexedrine, Epinephrine, Ephedrine)	Chemical synthetics	Orally Spray	"Pep" Excitement Delirium Dispels fatigue	Stimulant; not as dangerous as others; abuse results in chronic intoxication; may lead to psychosis; called "modern cocaine"; non-narcotic
Barbiturate (Barbital, Seconal, Allonal, Nembutal, Veronal, Luminal)	Barbituric Acid	Orally Pills Tablets	Soporific Overdose is fatal Intoxicant	Depressant; non-narcotic
Alcohol (Ethyl)	Chemical	Orally	Slows down activity	Affects coordination; depressant

(*n*) = Narcotic
Other common synthetic narcotics: Pantopon, Methadone, Metapon, Nisentil, Amidone, Beridone, Dromoran, etc.

fifty universities, only one percent of the students had taken LSD. At the other extreme, a student at a western state college (himself a drug-user) claimed that between forty and fifty percent of the student body had tried LSD.

As Lerner points out, there are no significant statistics available for precisely the same reason there are no facts available on virginity.[17] Students aren't talking. Yet no one questions the fact that drug-taking is becoming increasingly popular on college campuses in the United States.

The most common drugs selected by college students are marijuana, LSD and the old favorite, alcohol. Marijuana and LSD are

17 Jeremy Lerner, "College Drug Scene," *Atlantic*, 216:5, November, 1965, p. 127.

recent additions to the college scene, while alcohol has been around for a long time. It might be well to discuss these three in more detail.

ALCOHOL AS A NARCOTIC DRUG

It may surprise some to see that alcohol is included among the drugs. Yet alcohol is certainly a narcotic drug. The difference is that it has become acceptable and popular. In a recent White House Conference on Narcotics and Drug Abuse, alcohol was named as the "outstanding addictive drug in the United States."[18]

The term *addictive* is usually reserved for drugs which create a physical dependency in the user. This means that, in order to feel reasonably comfortable and not experience withdrawal pains, he must have the drug with some regularity. Oftentimes a person takes a drug for "kicks" or for a momentary thrill. Once he has become addicted, however, in the sense of being physically dependent upon the drug, he takes the drug to escape the violent physical and emotional anguish which comes as a result of not having the drug. In the language of the addict, he is "hooked."

Normally, a person does not become "hooked" on alcohol. Social drinking is an acceptable part of our society, and it is the person who does not drink that is oftentimes considered to be a bit strange. Yet one can become addicted to alcohol as surely as one can become "hooked" on morphine. The number of alcoholics is mute testimony to this.

Contrary to popular belief, alcohol is a depressant rather than a stimulant. It gives the impression of being a stimulant because of its selective action upon the nervous system. The first part of the brain affected by alcohol is the area of the cerebral cortex which acts to restrain our more primitive impulses. This gives the impression of stimulation since we may become witty, eloquent and charming. Rather than being stimulated, we are only more inhibited. In fact, we are in the process of slowing down, a process that can lead to unconsciousness and in rare cases death, if carried to extremes. "Alcohol is a protoplasmic poison with a purely depressant effect on the human nervous system," says DeRopp in his book, *Drugs and the Mind.*[19]

[18] *Ibid.*, p. 128.
[19] R. DeRopp, *Drugs and the Mind* (New York, 1957).

Many persons who become addicted to alcohol are those who are seeking an escape from reality. As the nervous system, under the influence of increasing amounts of alcohol, becomes more and more depressed, the cares of the world slip away. A person is "hooked" on alcohol when he can no longer get along without it, which is much the same condition in which the heroin user finds himself. The difference is•that for the alcoholic the need is primarily psychological, while for the heroin addict, the addiction is primarily physical.

It is not so much the use of alcohol that presents a problem on college campuses, it is the misuse and the abuse. No one is certain of the number of "problem drinkers" in our country, but estimates range all the way from 4,500,000 to 10,000,000!

Mrs. Marty Morin, head of the National Council on Alcoholism, calls alcoholism an iceberg disease. "Statistically, alcoholism ranks as the fourth major health threat in the nation, behind heart disease, cancer, and mental illness, but it may well be No. 1 and just not show."[20]

No one is sure what causes a person to become an alcoholic. Some rely upon psychological explanations, and others favor chemical causes, such as vitamin deficiency, cholesterol concentrations, and hormone imbalance. Perhaps the best advice for a person who has no objection to drinking in moderation but doesn't relish the possibility of drinking to excess would be "Never take a drink when you *need* one!" Moderate users drink for pleasure. When they drink to escape, then disaster may be near.

For the mature college student, the decision to drink too much and too often must be considered in the light of the consequences of the act. Oftentimes, however, drinking too much is not a rational decision. Romantic as it is in the movies, few students start out to get drunk. "Monday next, wind and weather permitting," said the Duke of Norfolk in 1703, "I purpose to be drunk." Unlike the Duke, most students who drink too much drift into it, with little concern for wind, weather, or the day of the week. Perhaps an explanation for this drift could be found in the boredom and aimlessness which accompanies the dissatisfaction with one's own life. Drinking to excess then becomes something to do.

The responsibility for the act must rest with the individual. Is

20 *New York Times*, April 29, 1966.

he willing to live with the consequences of excessive drinking? Is he willing to face an 8:00 A.M. class with a hangover? Is he willing to spend weekends in a bar somewhere, or spend his energies trying to avoid being caught drinking in the dormitory? Oliver Wendell Holmes, in his poem "On Lending a Punch Bowl," put it well:

> 'Tis but the fool that loves excess;
> Hast thou a drunken soul?
> Thy bane is in thy shallow skull,
> Not in my silver bowl.

MARIJUANA, EARLIEST KNOWN HALLUCINOGENIC DRUG

It has been called *hashish* in Arabia; *beng* in Persia; *kif* in Morocco; *dagga* in South Africa; *charas, bhang,* or *gangha* in India; *marijuana* in Mexico; and in the United States, *marijuana, mary jane* or *pot.* Scientists call it "the flowering tops of the female plant of *Cannabis sativa.*"

No matter the name, marijuana has a long and colorful history as one of the earliest known hallucinogenic drugs. Norman Taylor, in his book, *Narcotics: Nature's Dangerous Gifts,* states that the drug was first described in 2737 B.C. by Shen Nung, a Chinese emperor. Throughout history, individuals have left records of their adventures with marijuana. Today it is becoming increasingly popular on college campuses in the United States.

Unlike other drugs discussed in this chapter, marijuana is not an addictive drug. One does not develop a physical dependence upon the drug so that it would be difficult to give it up. There is only a slight tolerance effect, meaning that if one uses the drug regularly he can get about the same "kick" with about the same amount. In fact, in the words of a psychologist studying the effects of drugs: "Marijuana is not a particularly harmful drug in terms of the pharmalogical effect . . . of all the poisons we take (including alcohol and tobacco) marijuana is the least harmful."

The user of marijuana soon finds that if taken in excess it can produce anxiety and nausea. As a result, the habitual user avoids excessive smoking. However, psychotic episodes are not unheard of among experimenters with the drug, although they are rare.

Marijuana has long been popular with musicians. They seem to be convinced that they play better under its influence. Controlled research has demonstrated, however, that when the musicians are under the influence of marijuana the music sounds worse.

Some of the "mystique" which has attached itself to the use of marijuana is aptly captured in these words of two musicians, M. Mezzrow and B. Wolfe:

"To us a muggle (reefer, cigarette) wasn't any more dangerous or habit-forming than those other great American vices, the five-cent coke and the ice-cream cone, only it gave you more kick for your money . . . all the puffed-up strutting, little people we saw around, jogging their self-important way along so chesty and chumpy, plotting and shaming and getting more wrinkled and jumpy all the time, made us howl. . . . We were on another plane in another sphere compared to the musicians who were bottle babies, always hitting the jug and then coming up brawling after they were loaded. We like things to be easy and relaxed, mellow and mild, not loud or loutish, and the scowling chin-out tension of the lush hounds with their fake courage didn't appeal to us."[21]

It would be difficult, if not impossible, to make a damaging case against marijuana except for three factors: First, the possession of marijuana is against the law. A person may find himself sentenced to five years or more in jail for possessing it. He may also be heavily fined.

Secondly, as is the case with most drug users, those who are attracted are least prepared to handle the consequences which follow. There is a certain "group" effect which is common with the use of marijuana. Few people smoke pot alone. In the group situation and under the calming, mellowing effects of the drug, individuals may commit acts which they normally would avoid. I am not here referring specifically to criminal acts. There is little evidence that crime is caused by smoking marijuana, although many people who smoke marijuana also commit crimes.

Marijuana seems to create a certain amount of sexual excitement. Smoking pot is normally simultaneous with a relaxing of moral inhibitions or standards. A young girl who sets out to have a high time smoking pot may find herself pregnant without having had the chance to consider that possibility beforehand. Certainly, under the circumstances of marijuana intoxication, one would not be able to thoughtfully consider the possible consequences of sexual intercourse.

[21] Jeremy Lerner, *op. cit.*, p. 128.

In addition, when one smokes marijuana his powers of judgment in time, space and powers of reasoning are impaired. If driving a car, a person may attempt to avoid an object by swerving quickly even though the object may be a block away. A mother may be convinced that she has recently fed her baby even though hours have passed.

Finally, smoking marijuana can become escape from reality. As has been mentioned earlier, occasionally escaping from reality cannot be considered "bad." We all do it. But the problem of habitual marijuana smoking lies in the habit of escape when faced with problems. As Charles Winnich, director of the Narcotics Program of the American Social Health Association, has stated: ". . . the most insidious effect of marijuana may be the 'habit of tuning out' on reality when reality appears to offer discomfort."[22]

LSD: WHAT IT IS AND WHAT IT DOES

Perhaps the most talked-about drug on the college campus, and elsewhere, in recent months has been lysergic acid diethylamide (LSD). LSD is one of the most potent substances known to man. As little as one ounce can provide "trips" for 300,000 persons.

It is derived from a fungus called ergot, a parasite which grows on rye. LSD was discovered by a Swiss chemist, Dr. Albert Hoffman, in 1938. It was not until 1943, however, that he stumbled upon the "consciousness-expanding" properties of the drug by accidentally taking a small amount and experiencing a full-blown reaction.

During the late 1940's and 1950's the drug was considered an important weapon in the fight against mental illness. Since the reaction to the drug is closely related to the psychotic experience of a seriously ill mental patient, it was reasoned that one could come to understand and therefore assist the disturbed person.

After much experimentation and research, psychologists and psychiatrists are not as optimistic as they once were, though there are those who have claimed impressive results in treating schizophrenics and alcoholics with a combination of LSD and intensive psychotherapy.

The reaction to LSD is based upon changed chemical conditions of the nervous system. Some claim that LSD alters the chemistry of

22 Fred Hechinger, "Drugs on the Campus," *New York Times*, May 15, 1966.

the cells in the brain. Others are more cautious. There is general agreement, however, that under the influence of LSD, the world and all in it change dramatically. The process of perception is especially affected. Minute details become central and important. Cracks in the paint, ignored before, become overpowering. A mole on a person's face dominates the room.

A person's behavior also changes. One experiences dissociation and detachment, a sense of being removed. As a result, his judgment is impaired and he tends to act on impulse. He often experiences a sense of personal superiority and combines it with a religious and philosophical solipsism. He is prone to attacks of laughter as well as periods of intense and horrible fear. In short, his world of experience is drastically changed.

As far as is now known, LSD is not an addictive drug. It builds no physical dependency in the user. It does create a high tolerance however. This means that if a person takes LSD for three days in a row, the third dose must be considerably larger than the first in order for the person to experience the usual effects.

THE DRUG USERS

Not all students on college campuses experiment with drugs. In fact, the number seems to be quite small. Two groups of students can be described which may be expected to take a drug.

The first group, and the larger of the two, consists of students seeking to do something forbidden. Ten years ago it may have been organizing a panty raid or water fight, or perhaps some sort of fraternity foolishness. Today, as the fraternity declines in importance on the college campus, the student tries pot or LSD. He experiences a thrill of sorts, an adventure in doing something wrong.

One of the tasks of adolescence is to establish an identity, a sense of self-understanding and self-worth. Part of this task consists in becoming independent from one's parents. Certain kinds of rebellion against parents seems to facilitate the process of self-understanding and, in a sense, contributes to the educational process.

The second group of drug users combine the sense of pleasure gained from participating in an illegal, rebellious activity with a general protest against the American society and its values. This group is much smaller. These students are disillusioned with society;

yet they choose a method of protest which is not in any way constructive. It has been noted that volunteers for the Peace Corps have seldom been involved with drugs. The reason seems to be that, even though they protest against traditional policies and procedures, they attempt to channel their protest through constructive action.

A sociologist named Kenneth Keniston has described modern-day college students by dividing them into two groups, the Professionalists and the Deviates.

The Professionalists, says Keniston, value technical, intellectual and professional competence above popularity or belongingness. They seldom became involved in issues and tend to play it safe. They cannot afford to risk themselves since so much depends upon good academic records and entrance into professional and graduate schools. There would seem to be little chance that these students would experiment with LSD or any other drug.

The Deviates are divided into three sub-categories, the Activists, the Disaffiliates and the Underachievers. The Activists, according to Keniston, are committed to specific issues. Their protests take the form of personal expressions of moral indignation against situations they consider to be intolerable. One probably would find drug users among this subgroup, but they would tend to be those who tried it for the excitement or for a demonstration of rebellion, or perhaps because others in the protesting group encouraged them.

The Disaffiliates are the escape artists. They want little to do with a conventional society which has, in their opinion, failed them. Their protest is a repudiation of all that adults stand for. It is within this group that one would find most of the drug users. Drugs are considered by them as ideal methods for denying the existence of a world toward which they feel no responsibility or affection. They long for the calm, muffled world of pot or the bizarre "trips" with LSD.

The third group under the Deviates is the Underachievers. These students, in addition to rejecting their society, as do the Disaffiliates, also reject themselves. Their search for meaning becomes more arduous and pessimistic. Members of this sub-group may also use drugs, but their reasons would tend to be entirely escapist in nature with little or no protest involved.

There may be another group, in addition to the Disaffiliates, which attracts many student users of drugs. This group belongs to the Intellectual sub-culture of the campus. Its objective is not escape or protest as such, although oftentimes its members are in the vanguard of any demonstration, but experience. "We must experience all things," they say, "in order to understand our world." These students emphasize the consciousness-expanding characteristics of drugs—especially LSD—and claim remarkable and unusual insights into the meaning of truth, beauty, and the universe. Their claim is often a pseudo-scientific one in that the taking of drugs is justified in the name of science. Taking drugs becomes another intellectual adventure in which to participate. The learning to be achieved is sufficient as a reason for the act. These students are oftentimes heard to state that they would try LSD at least once for the experience.

I recognize that all categories into which students are put are partially invalid. Yet this analysis of student sub-culture, brief as it is, may serve to point out that certain kinds of students are more prone to using drugs than others.

WHY STUDENTS USE DRUGS

Why do college students use drugs? This question, like most questions that are important and worth asking, has no simple answer. I have already alluded to reasons which may prompt a student to experiment with drugs, or even become a habitual user. The rebelliousness of youth is often cited as a reason. Students find meaning and satisfaction in doing illegal and sometimes bizarre things (like swallowing goldfish) because it helps them to see themselves better in relation to authority. The drug user has a ready-made identity in relationship with others who also use drugs. LSD can be a "magic" solution to the developmental problems of young adulthood.

Other students may be escaping from their "too much" world and find their "cool" in the never-never land of half-dreams and uninvolvement. Still other students may be so disappointed and disillusioned with themselves that they decide it isn't worth the struggle and "leave the field."

Let me quote from a student who takes drugs:

"Why do we try drugs? We really feel we're limited so much. And we want to do so much and we're always told we should try things and grow.

It seems hypocritical of older people to tell us not to try certain things. We feel we can take care of ourselves. . . ."[23]

This student speaks for those who claim that experience, in its pseudo-scientific disguise, is a legitimate reason for taking drugs.

Part of the problem undoubtedly lies in the technical, impersonal society which we have created but cannot understand. We feel lost and meaningless in the face of huge questions which have outmoded answers. Religion no longer serves us. Science cannot win our loyalty and trust. We feel abandoned and alienated, "lonely and afraid in a world we never made." Our search for meaning has led some of us to psychiatry, others to Zen, others to absolute resignation and despair, and still others to drugs.

Our ancestors found meaning in the soil, in their God and in their families. Today, we have no soil to till, our God is dead, and our families are separated, each member living in his own particular peer-group-oriented society.

Yet, are these conditions of our present day society sufficient reasons for taking drugs? Probably not. In the complex, inter-relatedness of modern life it is difficult to separate causes and consequences. We are unsure which are the symptoms of a disintegrating society and which are the causes.

Others present more straightforward reasons for drugs on the campus. David Laskowitz, in a book entitled *Drug Addition in Youth*, believes that one of the underlying motives for the use of drugs is a reluctance to defer immediate gratification. In a world overshadowed for twenty years by the Bomb, many young people adopt a "here-and-now" rationale. "Since we may not be around tomorrow, let's live today," they seem to say.

Fred Hechinger, education writer for the *New York Times*, is of the opinion that one of the most fundamental causes of increased use of drugs among college students is a combination of overly-permissive parents and a speed-up of experiences for youngsters. "The rushing of adolescence (or elimination of childhood) permits increasing numbers of youngsters to experience earlier partying, dating, sexual experimentation, smoking, drinking."[24] As old thrills wear off, he thinks, the search is on for new ones. Many of these new thrills center about the use of drugs.

[23] Jeremy Lerner, *op. cit.*, p. 127.   [24] Fred Hechinger, *op. cit.*

No one knows the real reasons that students have turned to drugs, least of all the users themselves. One can only speculate. One thing is certain, however, the complexity of the causes is staggering. There are no simple answers here.

DANGERS IN USING DRUGS

In April of 1966, Dr. James F. Goddard, Commissioner of the Food and Drug Administration, sent out a letter to all colleges and universities in the country expressing grave concern over the increased use of drugs on college campuses. He stated that action must be quickly taken or else "an untold number of our students may suffer permanent mental or physical injury."

There is considerable evidence that supports Dr. Goddard's conclusion that using drugs may be injurious to physical and emotional health. There are many verified reports of cases where the taking of a hallucinatory drug triggered a latent psychosis. The experience of the drug proved to be damaging enough to send the individual over the brink.

Three psychiatrists at the New York University School of Medicine report that indiscriminate and widespread use of hallucinogenic drugs has resulted in increased hospital admissions for patients suffering adverse reactions to them. Of the twelve patients they treated, seven had acute panic reactions; three suffered reappearance of "drug" symptoms long after having taken LSD; and three developed prolonged overt psychoses.[25] Other researchers report similar findings. Hallucinogenic drugs have an enormous and unpredictable impact on the physical and emotional equilibrium of an individual.

I once attended a lecture on hallucinogenic drugs and asked the expert if there were any reason for not taking LSD at least once for the experience. He considered his answer for a moment and then replied that he saw no reason for gaining this sort of experience. The effect of LSD is a temporary psychotic state. "Why," he asked, "would anyone want to become psychotic, even for a little while?" Experts point out that the taking of these extremely potent and dangerous drugs without adequate control and supervision is a pharmacological form of Russian roulette.

[25] *Scientific American*, February, 1966, p. 54.

A woman, after suffering a siege of acute paranoid schizophrenia, was given LSD in conjunction with intensive and prolonged psychotherapy. "If I hadn't had the preparation," she stated, "I would never have come back. Because the fear was so deep . . . I would have been so frightened." Her treatment was highly successful. It is important here to emphasize that she was administered LSD only after careful and prolonged preparation.

Another serious danger in the indiscriminate use of drugs on campus lies in the area of value systems. Specialists have observed that "LSD seems to affect a person's value system. In many instances formerly productive individuals have adopted the attitude that one should live merely for the subjective experience, and not play various 'games'—like work—that society demands."[26]

They observe that mental health is often defined as the ability to work, to love and to play. It is in these very areas that users of hallucinogenic drugs tend to deteriorate. Habitual users seem to lose interest in work or play and tend to withdraw from people.

Dr. Dana Farnsworth, a psychiatrist at Harvard University, sums up the dangers of drugs with these words:

. . . once vulnerable students start taking drugs their whole lives seem to revolve around them. Since their preoccupation is incompatible with studying, many of them fail in their work. The greatest danger is not among graduate students but among adolescents 16 to 20 years of age who are often full of despair, uncertainty and anxiety, a mark of their age and their time.[27]

In this chapter I have attempted to present objective evidence concerning the effects of using drugs—primarily LSD, alcohol, and marijuana—while attending college. It was assumed that you, the reader, would make up your own mind whether or not to experiment with the drugs. The mark of the responsible person is his willingness to accept responsibility for his own actions. Therefore, it is also assumed that you will accept any consequences. But one cannot intelligently make decisions about future conduct without knowledge of the possible consequences. I hope that this chapter has provided knowledge about the effects of using drugs.

---

[26] J. Thomas Ungerleider and Duke D. Fisher, "LSD, Research and Joy Ride," *Nation*, 202:20, May 16, 1966, p. 575.
[27] Fred Hechinger, *op. cit.*

If I may be permitted a personal note, if someone were to ask my advice regarding LSD, or marijuana or the excessive use of alcohol, I would advise against it. As a psychologist, I have been unimpressed by the testimony of those who claim that the meaning of life has been revealed to them under the influence of drugs. I have been impressed, however, by the evidence of psychiatrists, physicians and psychologists, who have stated that these drugs contain potential dangers to physical and emotional health. The words of Dr. Farnsworth are worth considering carefully:

People who are attracted to the hallucinogenic drugs are often those most likely to be harmed by them. . . . Latent psychotics are disintegrating under the influence of even single doses. . . . Habitual use of the drug will lead, in some individuals at least, to looseness in thinking and difficulty in communicating coherently. One individual known to the writer can hallucinate at will, without resorting to the drug.[28]

As an educator, I am convinced that the user of drugs is missing much of what can be learned in college. He usually withdraws from the experience of college in favor of his own introspective existence. At the same time he runs the risk of being asked to leave college because of being caught with drugs or because of irregular studies. Also, he is in real danger of legal complications, which could result in a jail sentence if he is apprehended with drugs in his possession. He doesn't even have to take the drugs to be found guilty.

Before ending this chapter, I should like to introduce you to David, a bright college student. David was bored and unimpressed with his college life and so turned first to alcohol, then to marijuana. Neither satisfied the need he felt to be "jolted."

There had to be something that would shake me. No people were shaking me, no ideas were shaking me and no course was shaking me, and no experiences were shaking me, so I said, What can shake me? LSD maybe. So I thought I'd try LSD to see if it shakes me into something new.[29]

David visited a friend who had been high on LSD for five days. The friend gave him a cube of sugar which was impregnated with a double dose of LSD.

So I took the cube. For a while it was nice. I'd lie down on the bed, hear some music and the music would sound nice. I'd see pretty colors

[28] Quoted in Jeremy Lerner, *op. cit.*, p. 134.   [29] Jeremy Lerner, *op. cit.*, p. 130.

dancing on the wall. But the fact that new and completely different, if not contradictory, ideas kept popping up in my mind, gradually began to depress me. I'd jump into one thing, then I'd say no, that's wrong; then another thing, then no, that's wrong . . . and when I started to feel my mind flipping out of my body, I thought, Jesus Christ, I don't care how simple the pleasures would be, I'd rather be *back there*. I'd rather be in a boring state than where I am now because I cannot live this way. I don't want to be like this. I'll commit suicide, if necessary. I thought that this was going to go on continually and I just couldn't cope with it.[30]

But need our lives be so uninteresting and flat that we seek excitement and thrills or escape in drugs? "If your everyday life seems poor to you," wrote Rilke in his *Letters to a Young Poet*, "do not accuse it; accuse yourself, tell yourself you are not poet enough to summon up its riches, since for the creator there is no poverty and no poor unimportant place."[31]

[30] *Ibid.*, p. 133.
[31] Quoted by Abraham Maslow, "Lessons from Peak Experiences," Richard Farson, editor, *Science and Human Affairs* (Palo Alto, 1965), p. 47.

6 / *William J. Bowers*

CONFRONTING COLLEGE CHEATING

If you are an "average" student attending an "average" college, you probably have seen another student cheating during a test or examination; you have a 50-50 chance of knowing about a cheating incident in at least one of the courses you took last term; and it is only slightly less likely that you have been approached by another student for help during a test or exam.

These are results of research conducted with more than 5,000 students on 99 college campuses.[1] They clearly indicate that most college students will encounter cheating on their campuses. Although students may wish to ignore it, cheating will occur and will have its effect on them and their peers.

The belief that some colleges are more successful than others in controlling cheating led to this nationwide study of academic dishonesty. The study was designed to discover several things: the conditions under which cheating occurs; the pressures that make some students resort to cheating; the constraints that enable others to resist these pressures; and how cheating may be successfully controlled and reduced on the college campus.

The findings are important for the student who encounters cheating. To take a responsible approach to the problem, he must be aware of the sources of college cheating and of its effects on those

[1] William J. Bowers, *Student Dishonesty and Its Control in College* (New York, 1964).

involved in it. Then he will be better prepared to consider how academic dishonesty relates to his own personal values and what he can do about it.

WHY DOES CHEATING OCCUR?

Suppose, for the sake of argument, that institutions of higher learning, like libraries or museums, made their facilities available to everyone without regard for qualifications or past performance. The student's decision about what to study and how long to continue in school would be entirely up to him. The only reward for his academic efforts would be the sense of progress and achievement he personally experienced—no credits, no grades, no diplomas given.

Cheating would have no place in such a system. Instructors would have no responsibility for judging the progress of their students, so students would have no occasion to deceive their instructors.

But most American colleges and universities, unlike libraries and museums, set standards of performance and evaluate students' work in terms of these standards. Colleges not only offer education; they see that it is acquired. For without the evaluation of student performance, higher education would be a costly and inefficient enterprise. Without grading, higher education could not play the prominent role it now does in channeling well-qualified students to positions of responsibility and influence in society.

Grading, however, is also supposed to facilitate learning. Presumably, instructors, by examining students' work, discover strengths and weaknesses. With this insight, the instruction can be adapted to the students' needs. Ideally, the evaluation should uncover any particular difficulties the students are having and motivate them to perform better in the future.

Once the instructor judges students' performance, cheating becomes a possibility. Whether it will occur depends partly on the way these evaluations are made. Deception may be quite difficult under some systems of evaluation. For example, an apprentice under the watchful guidance of a master craftsman will find it difficult to deceive the master.

Likewise, it will be difficult to deceive the faculty member who becomes familiar with many aspects of the student's work and takes great care in evaluating it. At most colleges, however, the instructor cannot afford to make such detailed judgments. He must judge the work of many students; he must base his judgments on but a small sample of what the student is supposed to know; and the grade he assigns must give proper weight to various aspects of the student's work. As faculty members will attest, the task is a difficult one; the judgment must be made quickly and often on the basis of superficial evidence. Such decisions are necessarily imperfect—open to error and deception.

The two principal kinds of work used for evaluation are tests given in class and papers or assignments prepared outside of class. To these, the instructor can apply seemingly objective standards of evaluation. Yet doing well on papers and exams and knowing the subject matter of the course are not necessarily the same thing. The student may do well not only by knowing the subject matter but also by representing the knowledge and work of others as his own. On tests and exams, he may copy answers; on papers and assignments, he may use words or ideas found in published materials or other students' papers as if they were his own. The opportunity for deceit arises with each evaluation.

Many find it difficult to resist these illicit opportunities. To quote from the research report:

Our data show that at least half the students in the sample have engaged in some form of academic dishonesty since coming to college. This is a conservative estimate for the sample, and an even more conservative one for the population of college students.[2]

Cheating was defined in a conservative way in this study. The fifty per cent who had cheated consisted of students who admitted having:

—Copied from another student during an exam
—Plagiarized from published materials on a paper
—Used crib notes during an exam, or
—Turned in a paper done entirely or in part by another student

Obviously, these actions do not constitute an exhaustive list of dishonest practices. If we had included other acts that "were questionable" or "borderline" in terms of academic dishonesty, the rate would go even higher than 50 per cent. No doubt, some students were un-

[2] *Ibid.*, pp. 193–194.

willing to admit cheating, though many did admit it. Moreover, we have reason to believe that cheating was more prevalent among those who failed to return the questionnaire than among those included in our sample.

PRESSURES TOWARD CHEATING

If grades served only as an indication of his academic strengths and weaknesses, the student would have little reason for cheating. Academic dishonesty would simply rob grades of their value to him.

At most colleges, however, grades have an importance to the student far beyond indicating the quality of his work. In addition, they are a public record of his academic performance, and they affect a number of important decisions about what he can and cannot do at present and in the future.

Important opportunities and privileges depend on academic performance. Good grades in a prerequisite course may help a student gain admission to an advanced course; good grades in his major field may enable him to enter the departmental honors program; good grades across the board may win him a scholarship or fellowship to help defray educational expenses. If he makes the "Dean's List" or the "Honor Roll," he may gain the privilege of unlimited cuts (a self-limiting privilege, since those who abuse it are apt to lose it). Poor grades, on the other hand, may subject him to considerable pressure. To stay in school he must maintain a minimum average. If his grades are near or at the minimum level, he may be placed on academic probation. This action often entails a restriction of privileges, or perhaps a prohibition against extracurricular activities until grades improve.

The student's academic performance also affects the impression others have of him. If his grades are low, his peers may take it as a sign that he is not very bright. Likewise, the student's grades will leave an impression on his instructors. Faculty members are likely to take particular interest in a student whose performance record is good.

Although most faculty members would deny it, their judgments can be influenced by the student's past performance and his reputation for good work. In the same way that good grades can work on a student's behalf, poor grades can stigmatize him.

The student's parents, too, will be interested in his academic performance; they will take pride in good grades and be disheartened by poor ones. Their concern about his future, if not their financial investment in his college education, may lead them to exert pressure for better marks.

Thus, a student's grades are a means to many important ends. Others accept the grades as an indication of the student's success and potential. In effect, his grades serve as a kind of social credit in his dealings with parents, peers, faculty, administration, and prospective employers. It is not difficult, therefore, to understand why students want to make good grades—why grades sometimes become an end in themselves.

This tendency for grades to displace learning as a goal may be why several of the nation's leading undergraduate colleges have "de-emphasized" grades, or at least turned away from a formal standardized system of grading. Instead, they have developed more informal and personalized procedures under which faculty members are encouraged to give more detailed criticism. Their evaluations remain a relatively private matter between the instructors and their students.

The pressure to improve their grades should be more intense among those whose grades are lower. Relative to their peers, these students may find the academic work more difficult, and they are more apt to fear the prospect of flunking a course. They may even have difficulty staying in school.

The data show that the poorest students are the ones most likely to cheat. Cheating steadily increases as academic standing decreases. Furthermore, poorer students probably feel increasing pressure to cheat as they proceed through school. They may become progressively more tempted to cheat to avoid flunking out.

The negative relationship between grades and cheating increases from the freshman to the senior year, indicating the cumulative pressure on the poorer student to engage in cheating in order to survive in college.

There are several ways for the student who wants to improve his grades to achieve that end. The most obvious is to devote more time and energy to his studies. Simply by spending more time on school work and completing all papers and assignments, he should be able to improve his performance. Time spent on studies, however, is time not available for other activities.

Of course, another alternative is to be more efficient about the time he does spend on studies. He may seek to improve his study habits—to develop his power of concentration, to organize his paper-writing efforts, and the like. These efforts will take time and energy, however, at least until they are perfected.

We have evidence that cheating is more prevalent among students who are unwilling to spend time and effort in meeting academic demands—students who do not want to adopt the legitimate means to the academic goals they desire:

The data . . . indicate that both time spent on studies and effectiveness of study independently affect the likelihood of cheating. Thus, whatever the number of hours they study, students who keep up to date on their course work are less prone to cheat than those who fall behind. And, at the same time, students who spend a great deal of time on their studies are less prone to cheat even when they have not mastered their work. . . . The largest concentration of cheating is to be found among those who take their role as student most lightly, those who study neither long nor efficiently.[3]

Yet the student need not rely on himself alone. His friends may be willing to tutor him and to help him develop more effective study habits. Students in his courses, particularly those who are doing well, may give him insights into the criteria the instructor stresses. Of course, by asking for help, the student acknowledges his weaknesses, and some find this quite painful.

Perhaps the best person to advise the student is the course instructor. After all, he is in a good position to know the student's academic problems. Approaching the course instructor, however, may be even more painful for many students than seeking advice from classmates and friends.

Aside from improving one's grades, a student may cheat simply to escape what he regards as excessive academic demands. Or, he may cheat in one course because he wants to study for another course which he thinks is more interesting or more important.

Or, if the student is seeking social success, he may feel that dating, athletics, and other extracurricular activities require most of his time and attention. Just as cheating may free time from one course for another, it may also release time to meet social demands.

In the words of the research report:

3 *Ibid.*, pp. 82–83.

In addition to the specific adaptation students make to academic demands, they make a more general adaptation to college itself, which is reflected in the relative importance they attribute to the intellectual and social aspects of college life. This distinction between intellectual and social value-orientations appears in the kinds of friends they choose, their major field of study, the goals of education they consider important, and their involvement in campus social life. Our data show that those who value the social aspects of college life are more apt to cheat than those who emphasize intellectual interests and activities, even when we take their academic performance into account. Presumably, students who place primary emphasis on intellectual matters are more committed to the academic life and more sensitive to the norms of academic integrity that govern it.[4]

Cheating may also be a response to frustration in college life. Some students feel that they are wasting time in college. This sense of dissatisfaction may be released in antagonism toward faculty and annoyance with other students. Cheating may be one mode of expressing this hostility.

CONSTRAINTS AGAINST CHEATING

We can now see what sets cheating in motion. There are possibilities for deceit in an imperfect system of evaluation, and there are many motives for academic dishonesty. So, what is there to stop it? The desire for better grades is common virtually to all students. Why, then, do many students *not* cheat?

Perhaps the foremost factor is a student's own moral stance on cheating—his feeling that cheating is wrong. Even though the student believes he could improve his grades by cheating, he is unwilling to take this step. His personal disapproval makes him stop short of dishonesty.

The students surveyed were asked how strongly they agreed or disagreed with the following statements about cheating:

—"The individual's personal sense of integrity or self-respect should be the basis of the decision not to cheat"
—"Students are morally obliged not to cheat"
—"Cheating directly contradicts the goals of education"
—"Under no circumstances is cheating justified"

[4] *Ibid.*, p. 195.

Students' responses reflect a definite recognition that cheating is wrong. More than four out of five students agree with each of these statements, more than three in five express a *strong* agreement. The disapproval of cheating reflected in these statements is a strong deterrent to cheating behavior.

As we move from strong disapproval (agreeing "strongly" with all four statements) to weak disapproval or tolerance of cheating (agreeing "strongly" with none of the statements) we find that the proportion of students who cheat increases markedly. . . . Just knowing how a student feels about cheating, then, takes us a long way in predicting whether he will engage in this kind of behavior.

The typical college student associates with other students who share his interests and activities and whose company he enjoys. These other students will put pressure on the individual to live up to certain norms of conduct. If the student accepts the values of his peers, he will win their approval; otherwise, he will feel their disapproval.

According to the research report:

. . . the disapproval of cheating that students sense among their peers has a strong relation to their cheating behavior. The stronger the disapproval they perceive, the less likely are they to cheat.

When peer disapproval is strong only about a quarter of the students cheat; when it is weak, almost three-quarters do. This relationship is as strong as any we have uncovered so far in the search for determinants of academic dishonesty.[5]

A student's immediate peer group is not the only source of constraint. He has a social existence and reputation outside of his own peer group, and this broader reputation will depend in large measure on his living up to standards of conduct shared by other students on campus. Although their feelings may not be as relevant to him as those of his immediate peers, he will nevertheless be sensitive to their opinions.

The evidence indicates that

. . . both kinds of social disapproval serve to deter academic dishonesty —the disapproval students perceive in their immediate interpersonal environment on campus, and the climate of disapproval characteristic of

[5] *Ibid.*, p. 147.

the student body as a whole. . . . A student's close associates seem to have a somewhat stronger impact on his behavior than do those more distant from him, but both sources of disapproval show a substantial independent effect.[6]

The climate of disapproval on campus may act as a constraint on cheating in still another way. It may facilitate efforts at control by faculty and administration. In other words, where the climate of disapproval of cheating is strong, institutional enforcement is apt to be more effective. A tougher approach to the problem of academic dishonesty by those in authority will be accepted as legitimate and appropriate.

Stronger formal control will, in turn, stimulate and reinforce feelings of disapproval among students. Becoming aware that cases are being discovered and observing that severe punishments are imposed will strengthen commitment to the norms among the great majority of students on the campus.

Under such circumstances, cheating becomes a much more risky business. The student who cheats is more likely to be caught and to be punished severely. Even if he is not caught by authorities, he is more likely to be subjected to informal sanctions from his peers. The student who is contemplating cheating may decide that an extra investment of time in his studies is preferable to academic dishonesty.

Just as formal and informal controls make cheating more risky for the would-be cheater, they also make it more risky for anyone who would help him cheat. Thus, a student who might come to another's aid when chances of being caught and punished are remote will be reluctant to do so as social controls become more effective. In other words, even if social controls fail to deter a given individual, they will still make it harder for him to cheat by depriving him of illicit opportunities which might otherwise be available.

The importance of peer disapproval may account for the dramatic success of honor systems on many college campuses. The research revealed that:

The level of cheating is much lower at schools that place primary responsibility for dealing with cases of academic dishonesty in the hands of the students and their elected representatives, as under the honor system, than at schools that rely on faculty-centered control or have a form of mixed control, in which faculty and students jointly participate. Honor systems are more prevalent at some kinds of schools than at others, and their presence makes a greater difference in the level of cheating at some schools than at others. But in all categories of school size and sex composition, schools with honor systems are less apt to have a high level of cheating than those with other arrangements for control. Moreover, the difference that the honor system makes in the level of cheating of the college is greater on the average, than the difference due to variations in school size or sex composition. Presumably, in return for the privileges and trust students are accorded under the honor system, they develop a stronger sense of commitment to norms of academic integrity and, thereby, a strong climate of peer disapproval of cheating emerges on the campus.[7]

WHAT ARE THE CONSEQUENCES OF CHEATING?

To understand the problem of cheating and to determine the reasonable reaction to it, not only must the student know why cheating occurs, he must also consider the consequences of cheating for the educational process and for himself and others involved in it.

How big a problem is cheating in college? How serious is it? Research data show that the magnitude of the problem is grossly underestimated by the members of the campus community.

Two and a half times as many students have cheated as study body presidents estimate, and more than three times as many have cheated as deans estimate. Even students themselves underestimate the proportion of cheaters in their midst; they tend to believe that only about half as many have cheated as their self-reports indicate.

Our respondents may have underestimated the amount of cheating at their college because much of it goes undetected. Our study revealed that only a small fraction of those who cheat get caught and punished, and that punishments of cheating and plagiarism are relatively lenient at most colleges. Seldom are students suspended or expelled for academic dishonesty. Yet, despite their conservative estimates, many deans and student body presidents concede that academic dishonesty on their campus constitutes a "serious disciplinary problem."

It is not only the prevalence of cheating or the difficulty in con-

7 *Ibid.*, p. 198.

trolling it that makes campus authorities consider it so serious; it is these things together with the fact that academic dishonesty contradicts fundamental educational values. Our institutions of higher education embrace a tradition of learning and scholarship that stresses conscientious scholarly endeavor and a scrupulous regard for the academic efforts and contributions of others. The college is therefore concerned not only with imparting knowledge and ideas, but also with instilling a sense of integrity about academic work. The prevalence of academic dishonesty represents a failure on the part of the college to achieve these fundamental educational goals.

Furthermore, cheating creates a number of practical problems for faculty and administration. It frustrates the instructor's efforts to impart knowledge and to engender respect for independent critical thinking among students. In addition, it requires that the instructor be a watch dog—always on the lookout for cheating whenever he gives tests or makes assignments.

For each case of cheating that comes up, an administrator, usually the dean, must learn all the relevant facts of the case, review the academic record of the implicated student, consult with the instructor in whose course the incident occurred, and get in touch with others who know the suspect and his academic work. All this effort robs the administrator of time and energy he might fruitfully spend on other matters.

Cheating creates a particularly demoralizing situation for honest students, since it deprives them of an atmosphere in which honesty alone pays off. To the extent that cheating prevails and goes undetected, students will receive credit for work that is not their own and rewards to which they are not entitled. When good grades go to students who cheat successfully as well as those who work diligently on their studies, the grading system loses its meaning. Also, if students are graded relative to one another—on the "curve"—each gain the dishonest student makes in his grades as a result of cheating will be at the expense of the honest students in the class. In the classroom, the honest student often faces an unpleasant situation. He is aware that classmates are cheating; some may even approach him for help. If he sees others bettering their grades by cheating, he will probably be tempted to do likewise. In effect, academic dishonesty deprives the serious students of the appropriate setting for intellectual growth.

The consequences for the dishonest student are even more obvious. He risks punishment by the authorities and disapproval from his peers. In addition, he risks becoming progressively lost in his school work. A majority of the students in our sample agreed with the statement "the student who starts cheating soon becomes lost in his course work." And he may fail to develop adequate techniques for coping with legitimate demands placed on him by other people in the future.

A tendency for individuals who rely upon deceit in one social context to do so in another is suggested by our finding that students who had cheated in high school were more likely to cheat in college than those who had not cheated in high school.

Jerome Ellison discusses the ways in which college cheating may lead to problems in the larger society. Calling it the "American Disgrace," he argues that:

> . . . The space age demands rockets that will work, and these are not produced by designers who won their A's in math by cheating. The surgeon at the operating table needs knowledge, not just a grade. There is an increasing number of fields where fooling with truth, either through incompetence or fraud, can produce disaster. If the repositories of knowledge have grown careless about the truth, we are undone. It is somewhat as if a nation backing its currency with gold discovered that its value contained only pig iron.

> Crookedness in politics, in public office, in show business, in commerce, in finance, in sports—all these are old stories to a realistic American public. They are commonly shrugged off as occurring too rarely for real concern, or as the work of an uneducated, pseudo-criminal fringe. But large-scale humbug in our seats of higher learning is far more serious. Here we train the nation's moral, intellectual, commercial, and professional leaders. Fundamental damage in these vital centers could in today's world climate produce a self-destructive spiral spinning us toward national suicide.[8]

Finally, there is reason to question the presumed advantage cheating offers in improving one's grades. The student may be willing to risk being caught and punished or even losing out on the subject matter of his courses in order to improve his record. Grades are that important to many students! Yet, we have no evidence that cheating actually helps students get better grades. In fact, cheating

[8] Jerome Ellison, "American Disgrace: College Cheating," *Saturday Evening Post* January 9, 1960, pp. 58–59.

is more prevalent among students with lower grades, a fact which suggests cheating may be a relatively ineffective strategy for getting better grades. Those who adopted it do not demonstrate the results claimed for it.

Of course, even if cheating does contribute in some cases to the student's grade average, his self-interest in the long run may be sacrificed. For apparent academic success in the present, he risks missing out on the essence of the educational process. His myopic obsession with grades may displace the more distant educational objectives. He may miss seeing the forest for the trees.

FACING THE CHEATING PROBLEM

What then does all this mean to the college student? Does knowing about the causes and consequences of academic dishonesty aid him personally in coping with it? Certainly it gives him a chance to think about the way in which cheating relates to his own values and commitments. It should also make him aware of the nature and dimensions of the problem.

He must face the fact that cheating is an individual and educational problem which he cannot avoid or escape by turning his head the other way. Each assignment, paper, and test that he turns in provides some opportunity for deception simply because the instructor's evaluations are by nature imperfect. Pressures toward cheating are ever present. Students are always under pressure to improve their academic performance. The grades they get stand as a mark of their academic worth, visible to faculty, friends, family, and anyone else who is interested. Thus, as a matter of course, all students confront opportunities and pressures to engage in academic dishonesty.

A student can take steps to offset these academic pressures. By devoting more of his time and effort to school work and by cultivating good study habits, he can often improve his grades. He may also get help with his academic problems from his campus associates and from his course instructors, if he is willing to acknowledge his need. Yet, these measures strengthen his resistance to cheating only to a minor degree. More important as a constraining force are the student's personal feelings of disapproval of cheating and the feeling of disapproval among his peers. His ideas and feelings about cheating will be influenced by what he hears from his parents, peers, teachers,

86   *William J. Bowers*

and perhaps even by what he reads about the causes and consequences of cheating. It is he, however, who will sift and weigh what
he hears and reads, who will make the decision to act, and who must
bear the responsibility of his action.

Cheating is hard to defend, especially if one takes a broad perspective on its consequences for the educational process and those
involved in it. Not many students would try to defend it on moral
grounds. As we noted, the great majority of students agree that the
student is morally obligated not to cheat, that under no circumstance
is cheating justified, and so on. Even if our discussion exaggerate
the unfortunate consequences of cheating for the educational process
and for society at large, there is little if anything to be said on its
behalf.

The student might reply that this is all very well, that cheating
is wrong, and that it should be avoided in principle; but that because in practice it puts the honest student at an unfair disadvantage
he must cheat as a matter of self-protection. To get back on an equal
footing with the dishonest student, he must resort to cheating
whether he likes it or not. Since so many students have cheated—
twice as many as students estimate—he has no other recourse. What
else can he do?

But let's take a more constructive view of the alternatives than
simply being satisfied with a rationalization designed to neutralize
the educational consequences and moral values involved. After all,
there is more to the student's confrontation with cheating than
whether to engage in it himself. He must also decide what, if anything, to do about the cheating of others.

On the campus where cheating is prevalent, therefore, the
student is not simply compelled to go along with it or to suffer the
consequences. Another alternative is open. He may seek to reduce
cheating, at least among those students he knows, by expressing his
personal feelings about it to those around him and by encouraging
them to take a responsible approach to cheating. Evidence indicates
that his influence will be felt.

To say that another student's cheating is that person's own business is a fallacy. Cheating is surely the business of all those it affects.
Considering the prevalence of cheating in college, this includes a
great many people. Since cheating produces a demoralizing climate
in which the pursuit of intellectual goals is frustrated for all students, the problem becomes every student's business. Every student

has something to lose. Every student therefore has the right—very likely the obligation—to do something about it.

If we see an injustice being done, should it not be a concern of ours, even if we are not personally involved, or feel we are not? Cheating so clearly imposes an injustice on those who abide by the rules of the game, that even if a student saw no personal gain in keeping the classroom honest, he should still attempt to do so on behalf of those whom cheating hurts, including, of course, the cheater himself.

The impact students can have on the cheating problem at their college will depend on their ability to create a climate of disapproval of cheating. Making their feelings known individually will have an important effect. To bring the full force of peer disapproval to bear on their campus, however, some organized action to establish and enforce norms of academic integrity is required.

Exactly what steps need to be taken on a given campus may be uncertain, but it is clear that the efforts of students are essential. According to Virginius Dabney:

Honor codes . . . frequently have proven to be a most effective means of curbing the spread of cheating. For any honor code to be successful, however, it is essential to create a climate of opinion among students, and especially student leaders, on behalf of honorable conduct in the classroom. Everyone concerned must understand the harm the cheater does to himself, to others, and to society.[9]

Although some schools will not be prepared for it, the honor system is clearly one step students can take to combat cheating. At some schools this has been a tremendously effective step. Among the 99 schools studied, those with honor systems consistently had the lowest levels of cheating.

Yet the honor system is not suitable everywhere. We have a great deal to learn about how to take responsible steps to reduce cheating effectively on different kinds of college campuses. We need to have bold and imaginative efforts to control cheating designed and put into practice on college campuses. We need also to study these programs when they are being set up and when they go into effect. In this way the efforts of a few of us can contribute to the welfare of us all.

[9] Virginius Dabney, "Cheating Can Be Stopped," *Saturday Review*, May 21, 1966, p. 77.

7 / *Ray F. Shurtleff*

PLAGIARISM: THE GRAY AREA

One of the major forms of academic dishonesty is plagiarism on reports, research papers, and themes. In an analysis of this aspect of cheating one should look closely at three factors: its literary and historical context, the various forms that plagiarism may take, and the motives involved.

An examination of the history of plagiarism greatly involves the history of literature. Many of the great men of literature have been accused of plagiarism at one time or another, including such immortal figures as Plutarch, Sophocles, Aristophanes, Milton, Ben Jonson, Voltaire, and Shakespeare.

According to Rudyard Kipling in his *Barrack-Room Ballads* Homer also was suspect:

> When 'Omer smote 'is bloomin' lyre,
>   He'd 'eard men sing by land an' sea;
> An' what he thought 'e might require;
>   'E went an' took—the same as me![1]

Plagiarism in literature is therefore an established, but not necessarily accepted, fact.

In defining plagiarism, *Webster's Third New International Dictionary* expresses it simply to be "an act or instance of plagiarizing"

[1] Rudyard Kipling, *The Seven Seas* (New York, 1897), p. 144.

and defines the verb "to plagiarize" as "to steal and pass off as one's own (the ideas or words of another); present as new and original an idea or product derived from an existing source."

One source looks further into the etymology of the word. It is "suggestive of the thief, the pilferer. The Latin equivalent means a kidnapper, the Greek original means oblique, crooked."[2] Alexander Lindey, the author of an excellent book on the subject, goes a step further in stating that "Plagarism is literary . . . theft. It is the false assumption of authorship . . . the appropriation of the fruits of another person's mental labor and skill."[3]

FORMS OF PLAGIARISM

In a recent survey conducted at a large urban university by the Russell B. Stearns Study, faculty members were asked their opinions on various aspects of academic dishonesty. Of these participants 73.1 percent felt that "Turning in papers done entirely or in part by other students" was "Extremely Wrong"; 72.5 percent stated that "Writing a paper for another student" was "Extremely Wrong"; 62.3 percent expressed the opinion that "A student giving a term paper or report to a friend knowing he will copy it and turn it in as his own" was "Extremely Wrong"; 61.1 percent considered "Plagiarizing from published material on papers" as being "Extremely Wrong"; and 33.5 percent reported that "Copying a few sentences of material without footnoting it in a paper" was "Extremely Wrong." All of the above instances are acts of plagiarism, and this study helps to illustrate the severity of these transgressions.

A plagiarist will use various methods, willfully or unwittingly. Many times he is aware of the wrong he is committing; at other times he is oblivious of the fact. In a sense, plagiarism is a "gray area" as an ethical concern. There are no set rules or regulations concerning plagiarism, nor is there a specific answer to the question of what constitutes legitimate assistance and what constitutes improper aid; hence it is conceivable that a person can innocently plagiarize.

Plagiarism and its many aspects fall into four basic categories:

[2] Margaret C. Meagher, "These Plagiarists!" *Catholic World*, February, 1938, p. 590.
[3] Alexander Lindey, *Plagiarism and Originality* (New York, 1952), p. 2.

deliberate plagiarism, improper use of the paraphrase, use of outside help, and what can be termed "unconscious" plagiarism. These categories vary in their degree of gravity, but they are all reprehensible nonetheless.

DELIBERATE PLAGIARISM

Deliberate plagiarism can involve one or both of these acts: the lifting of sentences, paragraphs, illustrations, and even sections from a source for use in one's research paper, without acknowledgement in a footnote or in a list of references; or the alteration of sentences which omits the original author's personal thoughts.

Roland Wolseley, writing in *Saturday Review*, humorously discussed a proposed textbook for plagiarists and suggests tricks that a plagiarist might use, such as: copying from an obscure writer whose literary style might not be easily recognized; transcribing passages from a well-known writer but injecting one's own prose style into the material; borrowing phrases or paragraphs from the jacket cover of a book or perhaps a review of the book; and even the reproduction of words and ideas from a reference work.[4] In this devious form of cheating the plagiarist realizes he has committed a moral wrong, but he is trying to hide the flagrant violation. A student inexperienced in the ways and means of reporting may plead that he was not aware of his crime, but even this plea may fall on deaf ears. This form of literary appropriation can be detected rather quickly by an instructor if the style of the paper is significantly different from a student's previous work.

IMPROPER USE OF THE PARAPHRASE

One of the major rules of footnoting is that, if one uses a paraphrasing or an indirect quotation, it should be footnoted to the source whence it came. This rule, however, is disregarded by many students, either knowingly or through ignorance or simple carelessness. Lack of proper instruction as to the methods of footnoting will lead a student to unlawful paraphrasing and negligent note-taking, thus producing incorrect quotations and paraphrases.

[4] Roland E. Wolseley, "Plan For Plagiarists," *Saturday Review*, May 10, 1958, p. 25.

USE OF OUTSIDE HELP

The use of outside help can be an area of controversy. The free use of fraternity files on research papers, the copying of another student's term paper, monetary reimbursement to a fellow student or friend for writing a paper, are all serious plagiarisms. Each instance is an attempt to pass off another's mental labor and research as one's own. Having a friend review, criticize, and rewrite passages in a term paper is another form of plagiarism, since this procedure automatically decreases the originality of the paper. But if a friend makes grammatical corrections and suggests changes in style or wording, is this really a serious violation? True, it may decrease originality to a certain extent, but is it not more a part of the polishing-up process for a paper than a form of plagiarism? Many students may not consider this procedure to be a flagrant moral transgression. Professor Edgar F. Daniels elaborates on this matter:

Obviously, outside help can benefit the student; otherwise how justify having teachers? When is such help unjust? Few of us would be so dogmatic as to say it utterly unfair to the other students to hand one's freshly written theme to one's roommate for appreciation, even if the roommate offers some generalized comments on its readability. In fact, the value of such interaction would seem quite to outweigh the slight influence of the outsider upon the grade. Most of us would even countenance the extension of the friend's comments to problems of particular paragraphs, or even to sentences which seem awkward. But where does this legitimate assistance shade into the improper?[5]

Therein lies the problem. The limit of outside help, if there is any to be allowed, should be definitely stated to the student, as an instructor's thoughts on the mater may differ considerably from the student's.

UNCONSCIOUS PLAGIARISM

The last major category of plagiarism is probably the most often used mode of defense, that of the appeal to "unconscious" plagiarism. (After all, there is nothing new under the sun!) It most likely results from an imperfect scheme of note-taking, or a memory that is too exact, as a person may remember phraseology from a book he has

[5] Edgar F. Daniels, "The Dishonest Term Paper," *College English*, April 1960, p. 404.

read and not give credit for the idea or sentence. The conscientious student will take notes in an efficient manner, having every direct quotation in quotation marks and every paraphrase noted to the source. A great many students, however, write their notes as abstracts or summaries, and often omit quotation marks and even the source reference. The result is a research paper written with the use of incomplete notes and an inaccurate memory, a paper containing plagiarism that is due to "unconscious absorption." One editorial writer correctly recognized this problem:

Anyone who reads widely knows that his mind is stuffed with tags of plots, images, and rhymes. It is no sin to utilize such mental furnishings which become public property in the course of centuries, as the stimulus for a new creative combination.[6]

MOTIVES PROMPTING PLAGIARISM

Pehaps the most interesting component of a study on plagiarism is an analysis of the motives behind it. What moves a student to plagiarize willfully, or even innocently appropriate the fruits of another's labor? The reason for an innocent act of plagiarism might include one or more of these conditions: lack of proper instruction in note-taking, footnoting and the like; a lack of verbal ability, resulting in the use of a reference source as a crutch for faulty English training; and habits formed from previous research work, especially the frequent use of encyclopedias for high school reports. Yet there are explanations for willful piracy: the desire for money; the search for glory (praise from an instructor and fellow students); admiration of an author's writings; ignorance of pertinent laws, especially concerning copyright infringement; and possibly even psychological disturbance.

Ignorance and neglect cannot be the only basis on which the accused plagiarist may make a defense, for there are other influential factors. Some students simply lack the common sense to realize that proper research methods are not difficult to observe; hence they lean on their limited literary sources for their reports and term papers. Academic pressures, in the form of need for better grades and an overload of term papers in other courses, may turn a student to "borrowing." Realizing that a good paper will raise his course grade,

6 "This Is My Own Work," *Scholastic*, May 5, 1934, p. 3.

the student will appropriate the author's words and pass them off as his own verbal expression. Also because of lack of time owing to other commitments, a student will turn to literary piracy in order quickly and efficiently to complete his course obligations for a term paper.

Many times a student tends to brush off an accusation of plagiarism by saying that he sees little difference between this and other "subterfuges in life." Facts can be cited to support this argument. Public figures today make free use of ghost writers, and politicians often give speeches from material written by an assistant. Lindey best expresses the factors involved in the use of the crutch of past experience:

In a non-legal sense most of us plagiarize at one time or another. As young children we parrot the phrases of adults and are embraced for our precocity. We imitate our playmates in speech and behavior. In school we sometimes copy one another's homework. In college some of us make too-liberal use of reference texts in preparing our term papers and a few of us are not above cribbing at examinations. Grown up, we glean political views from newspaper editorials and radio commentators, and put them blandly forward as our own. . . . The point worth noting is that here, as in other areas of human conduct, the legal wrong—plagiarism—is a distant cousin, not a complete stranger, to a phase of our everyday behavior.[7]

There is yet another reason: the use of a common source in research, i.e., current events, past events, material drawn from the public domain, and other data. Similarity in facts and ideas is not necessarily a plagiarism, but similarity in modes of expression is.

William J. Bowers, in his analysis of academic dishonesty at the college level, brings out another pertinent factor concerning plagiarism:

For the individual, cheating, plagiarism, and the like may represent an emerging personality problem. It may reflect an inability to face legitimate demands placed on him by other persons. It would certainly seem to foster a disregard for socially accepted norms of conduct and to reinforce an inclination to find the "easy way" or to "get around" obligations he is supposed to accept and live up to as a member of society.[8]

[7] Lindey, op. cit., pp. 12–13.
[8] William J. Bowers, Student Dishonesty and Its Control in College (New York, 1964), pp. 3–4.

A further factor influencing plagiarism is the lack of ethics on the part of the student offender. Ethics involves one's moral principles and intellectual honesty. There should be honesty in the acknowledgement of literary sources (both language and ideas), since credit should be given where credit is due. The theft of a product of one's mind is not only a legal wrong but a moral wrong as well. The student who willfully plagiarizes thereby admits his lack of ethics. This weakness in ethical behavior can be partially attributed to the student's lack of knowledge as to the purposes of footnotes and the theory or scholarly documentation, as well as to a weakness in the moral fiber of the individual.

Plagiarism is a subject of great concern in the academic world, since the causes and the consequences of plagiarism are serious ones. The effects involve the future of our society and its leaders, inasmuch as values gained or lost will greatly influence college students. Although the faculty and the university play contributing roles, the brunt of the burden of decreasing plagiarism falls upon the shoulders of the student. He is the person who continues to find loopholes to avoid or evade honest research work, whether these attempts are deliberate or "unconscious."

Every college student and graduate should realize that he will probably need to write a number of reports at one time or another and that the more scholarly his presentations, the more benefits he will reap. His ability to produce a paper which satisfies the highest standards, both intellectually and ethically, can be to his great advantage.

8 / *Raymond O. Murphy &*
Charles W. Havice

EXTRACURRICULAR ACTIVITIES

Part One: The Invisible Curriculum

RAYMOND O. MURPHY

While he was president of Princeton University, Woodrow Wilson commented that student activities were the "side show that threaten to swallow the main tent."[1] In the fall of 1964 that prophetic remark became more poignant when a form of student activity—student political agitation—virtually paralyzed the Berkeley Campus of the University of California.

Colleges write their histories of student life in decade periods. As Clark Kerr, former president of the University of California, has aptly pointed out, each of these decades of college life is characterized by the excesses of student behavior in that period.[2] Thus, the 1930's were labelled the "Raccoon Coat Age" when in fact few could afford the luxury of a raccoon coat, if indeed the next semester's tuition. The 1960's have already been branded the "Activist Generation"

[1] Woodrow Wilson, "The Spirit of Learning" from an address before the Cambridge Phi Beta Kappa Chapter on July 1, 1909.
[2] Clark Kerr, "From Apathy to Confrontation," an address before the Conference on Students and Politics, sponsored by the Center for International Affairs of Harvard University, San Juan, Puerto Rico, March 28, 1967.

even though several studies indicate that only a very small minority of college students are ever involved in political activity while on campus. The image of the college campus as a jungle of protest placards and a sanctuary for all sorts of anti-establishment behavior is at direct odds with the impression of college administrators that student behavior has long since evolved through the worst of its excesses.

Dr. Kerr further indicates that the college is merely a reflector of the society of which it is a part.[3] Given our present world situation it is no wonder that political activities on the part of the student are their most highly publicized affairs. The point can also be made that changes in student life are most accurately reflected in student activities because, unlike any other aspect of the college, they are the only thing a student participates in voluntarily. For the most part the students themselves have developed, operated, and controlled the "Invisible Curriculum" of student activities. It is true that in the formal types of student activities such as student government, faculty and administrators have been assigned as "advisors." But then nobody has ever been sure about the proper function of an advisor.

Some of our American colleges are unquestionably more activity conscious than others, and recently we have been able to measure that fact. Others are more intellectually oriented and almost devoid of the adrenalin of student activities. One thing is certain. All colleges do have student activities. Furthermore, a quick glance at any college yearbook reveals that virtually every graduating senior has belonged to some organization or activity.

It is surprising how little is really known about student activities and their contribution to the development of college students. Equally interesting is the ability of many student activities to outlive their usefulness. On some campuses the annual effigy-hanging of the Dean of Students is still considered collegiate sport second in importance only to the athletic schedule. While faculty fret, approve, or withdraw from student activities, administrators are occupied in administering and philosophizing about them. Meanwhile, students are busy enjoying their activities.

The purpose of this selection is to briefly describe student activities on our college campuses, the present trends of these activities,

---

[3] *Ibid.*

and the reasons they exist (and therefore what one can expect to obtain from joining). It is hoped that this will assist the incoming student in making better decisions about student activities. The question is not whether you will or will not join. That matter has already been settled by the history of students before you. The concern should really be one of which and why, since in the "Invisible Curriculum" you will have the responsibility to exercise wise selection—a pattern of behavior your college hopes you will develop and utilize throughout your life. The "side shows" of student activities appear to be a rich offering of possibilities.

THE FORMS THEY TAKE

It is difficult to categorize student activities. In the broadest sense "student activity" is applied to everything a student does except attend lectures and study. With startling serendipity the category can include the now-infamous "panty raids" on a women's residence hall or a small group meeting in a residence hall lounge mentally wrestling with their professor over the question "What did Keats mean when he said. . . ."

We can, however, cull some sense out of the confusion if we consider two broad areas of student activity—the formal and informal. The formal student activities are those organizations and activities which are officially sanctioned by the college. The informal can be those activities of a more sensational bent (back to the "panty raids" and "quaking the Dean") which are by no means officially sanctioned. This second category should also include those activities which seek to become part of the formal structure of student activities—a group of students joining together to begin organizing a fraternity, for example.

The athletic program (both intercollegiate and intramural), fraternities and sororities, student government, publications, and the many forms of clubs constitute the formal strata of student activities.

Enough had already been written about the athletic programs of our colleges. Although we shall describe developments in student activities in greater detail, it is important to note here that a pronounced trend is for college students to become individually and personally involved in athletic activities. Possibly in response to a growing national concern for physical fitness we now find college students participating in athletic activity in an ever-increasing tempo. This participation ranges from the highly competitive fraternity-independent intramural events to coeducational athletic activities often dubbed "Powder Puff Derbys." The latter are intended more for laughs than for developing athletic prowess. It is reasonable to assume that the formal intercollegiate athletic schedule is only an iceberg indicator of the actual amount of athletic activity occurring on a campus.

Student government has begun to take new and interesting dimensions. This is probably a "back door" benefit of student activism. The "student activists" for all their bearded images and protests have made one unquestionable contribution to our college campuses; they have, perhaps unintentionally, served to strengthen the recognized forms of student government with which they are usually not directly associated. There is some hypocrisy often involved in the very term "student government" as it exists today. "Student government" might be more aptly termed "Student Administration" since there is precious little for them to "govern." Student government representatives spend the greater portion of their time in administering services and programs for their fellow students. A much smaller portion is devoted to advocating and working for changes in the status quo of student regulations. This is not to demean their contributions to the college. Most of our present programs and many of the services to students would not exist were it not for their efforts. When the ivy has crept up the spine of an encrusted administrator, it is the able and aggressive student leader who will "tell him how it is" and effect some important changes.

One of the characteristics of Americans is their urge to organize or as some wag put it "to clublicize." If something is "good" we will organize it. The college campus reflects this. The great bulk of student activities center around clubs. It is common for our large state universities to have as many as 400 clubs on the campus! These take the form of clubs with a specific academic orientation (The Shakespeare Club), those with specific religious commitment (Newman, Hillel, etc.), and those with specific political interests (Young Democrats, Young Republicans, Young Americans for Freedom, and the Students for a Democratic Society).

WHAT'S IN AND OUT

In 1963 the National Student Association, the national parent organization of many college student governments, published some interesting observations about student activities on the college campus.[4] I take the liberty of inserting my own observations taken from the context of a large state university. There is some support for such license. The large state university with its characteristic hordes of students often furnishes us with predictions of what will be found on smaller campuses in the coming years.

1. The movement of student activities is away from big group and all-college clubs to small group organizations where personal identity is possible.

Gone from our campuses are the annual puberty rites of spring called "May Day." Gone also are the massive proms with their accompanying sounds of "the big bands." Rapidly disappearing are the tribal-like war dances known as the "bonfire pep rally." Students have given up stuffing chicken wire with paper tissues to produce parade floats in favor of more serious intellectual activities. Numerous examples illustrate that there is a subtle sifting out from student activities of the unnecessary and frivolous. This movement away from mass-involvement activities is replaced by events which sometimes involve only a very few students. Ironically, many Deans of Students are worried that the "fun" has gone out of student activities. They almost nostalgically yearn for the days (and nights) they spent supervising parade float production and cooling the ashes of the campus bonfires.

It is unfortunate that a change of emphasis to intellectual activities often carries the connotation of grimness. I was relieved recently after having chastised one of our student leaders for his lack of academic achievement. Informed that he would be seriously curtailed in his extracurricular involvement until his average improved, he nudged me and with a glint in his eye said, "Don't worry, Dean, I'll still have a lot of fun around here." Wringing their hands over youth has been the traditional hygiene of elders. It helps their circulation.

[4] Wilton Pruitt, "College Students, Their Community, and Their Activities," *College Student Personnel Work in the Years Ahead* (Washington, D.C.: The American Personnel and Guidance Association, 1966), p. 13.

2. There is a growing revolt from and disdain for organizations whose primary purpose is self-perpetuation.

As previously indicated, alumni are often shocked to return to their alma maters to find many of the "sacred cows" of student activities no longer in existence. The notion of "prestige belonging" is slowly vanishing from the campus culture. Students are placing greater value on the inherent value of an activity rather than the name given it or its membership roster.

A persistent myth is that one must participate in student activities "for the record." Often the barkers of the "side show" are disappointed to learn that students do not respond to such superficial calls to join. There is no respectable evidence to indicate that employers of college students require participation in any given number of activities as a condition of hiring.

If our present college generations are able to enter the "outside world of reality" with the same degree of inquisitive candor, selectivity, and enthusiasm that they exhibit on the campus with respect to student activities, they cannot miss enriching their society.

3. Interest in student activities is becoming more polarized. The active are becoming more active, and vice-versa.

This is the sourest yet truest note in our observations of student activities. In terms of what student activities hope to accomplish they may be catering to the wrong students. Student leaders, for example, are quite unlike the students they represent. They already possess many of the characteristics that student activities hope to develop. Thus their participation may not really develop a particular trait but, instead, reinforce an already existing trait. There is a wide gap between the audience student activities hope to serve and those they actually do. Student leaders sense the problem. They complain often that they are unable to attract successors to these activities. A regrettable number of our college students with latent leadership qualities rationalize their non-participation with the notion that student activities are "cornered by the campus big men." Is it of any help to the potentially interested to say that such is hardly ever the case? There is always an acute shortage of excellence in any area of human endeavor.

WHY ME?

W. J. Burns has offered for your consideration a view of the values of student activities. "Its (student activities') contributions could help the student give up the familiar and reassuring, make choices and decisions, learn new patterns of conduct and thinking, break off old and establish new relationships, and above all help the student develop a valid concept of himself and his objectives."[5] Another writer, Dr. Kate Mueller, puts it somewhat differently in stating that student activities can teach a student to use his leisure time more profitably, reinforce what he learns in the classroom, provide him with the opportunity to test and modify his own personality with others, and help him establish higher standards and better values.[6]

Another important reason for the existence of student activities is that they can teach the democratic process. While most of our colleges are not themselves particularly strong models of democratic governance, they offer a quiet kind of sanctity in which students learn a great deal about the subtle inner-workings of the democratic order. In student government involvement the student will soon learn that the president of his college probably only "runs" the college on Monday mornings. The rest of the week is spent skillfully balancing the many counterforces that surround him.

Student activities further serve the purpose of perpetuating traditions on the campus. In so doing they provide healthy emotional outlets in an era when student life is often strained with competition. For as my academically stunted friend reminded me we must also place "fun" high in our value priority.

In essence, student activities offer the second track to becoming an educated man. It is not a question of whether the academic program should take exclusive precedence but of what the academic and student activity program can do jointly to produce an educated man. Student activities present the student with the opportunity to become more than he thought he would when he first enrolled at his college. And the process of "becoming" is what a college education is all about—becoming what you are capable of being.

[5] *Ibid.*, p. 15.
[6] Kate H. Mueller, *Student Personnel Work in Higher Education* (Boston, 1961), pp. 275–286.

The most obvious possible evil of student activities is excessive involvement. Countless legions have sunk in the quicksand of academia by majoring in extracurricular activities. But again, students are not to be frightened out of participation when we have evidence that our most outstanding student leaders also earn the best grades.

Within the activities themselves we find the limitations of human nature at work. Student activities are fundamentally social interrelationships. Some conscientious participants are clearly "worker bees" while the inert "drones" gather in the honey of publicity and esteem without much effort. That appears to be the human condition, and one should not be surprised to find it here.

The final salient pitfall of student activities is the question of selection. Exclusive participation in a narrowly selected interest group is self-defeating. More than one student has found his interests (and sometimes his vocational choice) altered by participation in a student activity that he "just tried." There should be a genuine spirit of adventure and inquiry as one approaches the selection of activities.

We began this essay by quoting a rather critical statement by Woodrow Wilson as President of Princeton University. We return now to the same source for a closing quotation:

"The real intellectual life of a body of undergraduates, if there be any, manifests itself, not in the classroom, but in what they do and talk of, and set before themselves, as their favorite objects between classes and lectures."[7]

Part Two: Fraternities, to Join or Not to Join

CHARLES W. HAVICE

One of the important questions that many college students consider is whether to enter the Greek-letter world. In America today, there

[7] Woodrow Wilson, *op. cit.*

are more than 20,000 chapters of men's and women's fraternities with a membership of around eight million. Beginning in 1776 with Phi Beta Kappa, then a social fraternity at the College of William and Mary, the fraternity system has grown in strength and influence in American life. The roster of fraternity members who have become distinguished leaders in all walks of life in our nation is most impressive. For instance, every President and Vice President of the United States born since 1825 has been a fraternity member, except two in each office.

POSSIBLE DISADVANTAGES

Before discussing the advantages of fraternity membership, let us take a look at some of the possible disadvantages which can cause the student to feel indifferent or even negative about joining.

Criticism has been leveled at some fraternities because their regulations bar some students on the basis of their race or religion. In a number of instances, such criticism has been entirely justified. However, in some cases the local chapter itself has protested against the national policy regarded as discriminatory. Occasionally, a chapter has withdrawn from its national organization in protest; occasionally, too, the central office has revoked the chapter's charter. The fact that the chapter had violated a rule may have justified such action, but the local group nevertheless may have demonstrated a higher ethical and social standard than did the national officers. To keep this issue in perspective, however, it should be noted that the instances of discrimination have been minimal. On balance, the fraternity system has been meeting the challenge of a new and better day in race and religious relations by modifying and liberalizing its membership regulations.

A second negative attitude concerning fraternity membership is the cost. Initiation fees, annual dues, badges, possibly blazers, and social functions are among the expenses. Costs differ from fraternity to fraternity and from campus to campus. Some houses admittedly indicate affluence and even luxury, but most of them are moderate and sometimes even modest in their level of financial operation. The following statement by the National Interfraternity Conference is informative concerning costs:

THE EXPENSE

With all its many advantages, fraternity membership might be expected to cost a great deal. Actually it is the biggest bargain in the educational field, representing less than 2% of an average college man's expenses.

This figure comes from a report of the United States Office of Education. A nationwide survey revealed that undergraduate members' outlays for their national and chapter fraternity dues amounted to 1.5% of total school expenditures at private colleges and 1.9% at tax-supported state institutions.

Fraternity living on many campuses costs less than in dormitories or private rooming houses. Few fraternities charge more. Generally speaking, an only added cost, aside from the modest pledge and initiation fees, is the monthly dues.

CAMPUS SUB-CULTURE

A third negative attitude about joining a fraternity is related to the changing sociological patterns in the campus sub-culture. It can be argued that living conditions are different today for many undergraduates. More of them are married, more very attractive dormitories and student unions are available, and an increasing number of students commute. Furthermore, some contend that the urge to join anything is less popular today. Many students feel that fraternity life has little value or meaning for them. Nevertheless, national fraternities have grown more than sixty percent since the Second World War and scores of new chapters are added each year.

A fourth criticism is the behavior of some fraternities. It takes only a few encounters with loud and profane language, drunkenness, wild parties, and juvenile rowdyism to convince the community that fraternities are a nuisance or worse. On the whole, fraternities consist of responsible, socially concerned students. They realize that they have much at stake in maintaining a good reputation, and resent the denigrating effects of the offending groups.

In addition to the above causes for apathetic or negative feelings concerning fraternity membership, there is the dilemma for some students as to whether they should join a local fraternity or a chapter of a national fraternity. On some campuses there is no choice the groups are all local or, less likely, all national. On most campuses the choice does exist. Yet it is a choice too subjective for any rule-of-thumb. However, there are many excellent local fraternities, and the fact that the fraternity being considered is not national should not be determinative.

IMPORTANT QUESTIONS

Much more important are the answers to such questions as these: Is it a group with whom daily companionship will be harmonious and even inspiring? What is the scholarship rating? What is its general standing and reputation on the campus and in the community? Bear in mind that a particular fraternity may emphasize some special interest, such as scholarship, athletics, social life, dramatics, journalism, and the like. Keep in mind also that the character and standards of a fraternity will have strong years, and weak years. Look before you leap. Investigate before you invest your life commitment, since you will find the fraternal bond is strong and lasting.

ABANDONING HAZING

Fraternity hazing or "Hell Week" has been an additional deterrent for some. Out of the millions of initiates there have been a few who have been seriously injured or killed. Of course, even one tragedy would have been one too many. Actually, hazing is rapidly being abandoned. The College Fraternity Secretaries Association frequently reiterates its opposition to hazing in any form. The week preceding the initiation ceremony is seldom a nightmare for the pledges. The psychological ingredients are retained—fellow-feeling among the put-upon initiates, obedience to their demanding superiors, and a sense of earning, through strenuous effort, the privileges of membership. But instead of hazing, constructive and beneficial duties are imposed. Collecting clothing in the community for a social service agency instead of collecting hub caps from car owners is one example of the change to desirable initiation practices. "Hell Week" has become "Help Week."

Let us now view fraternities in a distinctly favorable light. According to the National Interfraternity Conference, some of the reasons for joining the Greek-letter world are: Fraternities encourage superior scholarship and lessen the risk of being a dropout. More than half of all fraternity chapters are above the all-men's average in institutions reporting to the Conference. Chancellor W. Clarke Wescoe of the University of Kansas has said: "Fraternities have had a tremendous influence in improving scholarship." Fraternities increase by 42 percent the students' chance of graduating. Tom Harmon of football and sportscasting fame has said: "Without the interest and help of my fraternity brothers I might have been one of the unfortunates who didn't finish college. It was their interest and guidance that pulled me through."

Second, fraternities inspire high standards of conduct. Chief among the character values inculcated by fraternities is brotherhood. John Robson, authoritative editor of *Baird's Manual of American College Fraternities* has recently published a book *Educating for Brotherhood: Guidelines to the Meaning of Fraternity*. As its title indicates, the book makes central the meaning of brotherhood in its fullest sense.

SOME TESTIMONIALS

President Andrew D. Holt of the University of Tennessee has said about his fraternity experience: "It has given me brothers whose love and counsel I would never have gained without the bond." In similar vein Senator Hugh Scott of Pennsylvania acknowledged: "From the day I joined my fraternity until this day I have enjoyed a fullness of companionship and the joy of shared experiences which could have come to me in no other way."

IMPORTANCE OF RITUAL

Fraternities are built upon moral and spiritual ideas. Honor, honesty, and moral integrity are basic in the fraternal relationships. Of course, there are instances of moral defection. Drunkenness is sometimes a problem, despite regulations to encourage sobriety and temperance. The general influence and the total effect of fraternity life, however, is on the side of constructive and healthy idealism. Ernest R. Breech, Chairman of Trans World Airlines, probably speaks for many when he says, "My fraternity gave me moral and religious guidance and a good start in college."

HANDLING SUBTLE BALANCES

Third, fraternities develop leadership qualities and community-mindedness. Within the structure of the fraternity many opportunities are given the individual member to grow in the art of getting along with others, to develop self-confidence, to exert influence, and to emerge as one who can handle the subtle balances between leadership and followership. The fraternity also encourages the student to participate in extracurricular activities and to achieve leadership roles in them. Fraternity members furnish more campus leaders than any of the other campus organizations. Leadership experience at college offers a valuable foundation for similar responsibilities after graduation. Senator Mike Mansfield has said: "When men live and work together in a fraternal association, they enhance each other's capacity to contribute to the larger fraternities of community, state, nation, and world."

President Asa S. Knowles of Northeastern University recently made this observation at the annual convention of the Chi Psi fraternity:

A CLEAR CHALLENGE

"College and university enrollments are rising to unprecedented peaks across the nation. Enrollments of 25,000 or more are now commonplace at our large universities. Increasingly, college administrators are becoming concerned by the growing lack of opportunities for personal contact among their students. . . .

The challenge to the nation's fraternities is clear. They are uniquely qualified to provide the small social groups in which young men can come to know and live with others of similar interests. Our American heritage values highly a man's ability to work as part of a team. What better place is there than a fraternity chapter for a man to learn to live with others and work with them toward common goals and ideals? His brothers and advisers all contribute to the development of his personality. He learns the importance of loyalty to his brothers and that his own personal conduct reflects upon them. Not only does he develop scholastically, but he builds sound character and attitudes as well. His fraternity life is a preparation for leadership, and the chapter room shows him true democracy in action.

It teaches him parliamentary procedures, how to manage affairs, and the importance of tolerance and understanding.

. . . Fraternities will always exist at American colleges and universities. They meet a definite and urgent need."

9 / *Ronald E. A. Jackson*

RESPONSIBLE INDIVIDUAL EXPRESSION

The individual's right to express himself is one of his most important possessions. It is a valuable vehicle for developing as a person, and it is also a potent means of resisting tyranny, neutralizing obnoxious bureaucracies, and a basic tool for creatively reforming society and improving the human condition. The importance of individual expression as a force for recreating society cannot be overestimated.

In a theoretical sense, the right of the individual to express himself was established with finality for all Americans by the Bill of Rights. In practice, this right has been developing slowly throughout our history. At our country's inception the right of individual expression was truly available to only a privileged minority.

The gradual extension of this right to more and more sectors of our populace necessitated surmounting a variety of culturally imposed restrictions. Restrictions on individual expression have been based at one time or another in our history on sex, on status or power, on race, on age, and on moral tenets. They have been imposed on individuals, on groups, on classes, and at least in the case of Victorian restrictions, on ideas and expression—on virtually the whole of society. It is indicative of the continuous broadening and deepening of the meaning of democracy in our nation that public approbation slowly but surely has confirmed the right of individual expression for those sectors of our population formerly restricted by cultural precedents.

The passing of McCarthyism, the rise to prominence of colleges with their emphasis on academic freedom, the civil rights movement, the enhanced status and freedom accorded youth and the lessening of restrictive and constrictive ways of thinking about sex, morality, and theology have served to establish the privilege of individual expression for virtually everyone in our society.

As witness boisterous Berkeley, a true opportunity for the young to express themselves has been won only recently. This may account for what seems a peculiar posture often displayed by the majority of college students: many college-age youths appear to be engaged in a titanic struggle to gain the right to express themselves at just the time when that right largely has been secured. Youth's insistent demands for the right of individual expression today may simply be the over-zealous exercise of a newly acquired and not yet fully realized power.

CAMPUS DEMANDS FOR INDEPENDENT EXPRESSION

College students undoubtedly will continue to press their demands to secure independent expression for each of their number until the last remaining pockets of resistance are overcome. This mopping up is necessary and appropriate. However, in continuing to devote their attention primarily to a crusade that in most quarters has achieved its desired end, college students are running the risk of diminishing the public approbation they have so recently acquired. Even as they strive to strengthen their grasp of freedom of expression they simultaneously need to devote effort to acquiring those balancing characteristics of application which are required to make the exercise of this or any right both effective and also tolerable to others.

Analogously, it often seems that college students are practicing their right to express themselves as individuals in much the same manner as someone attempting to develop the power of a muscle. Their concern seems to be only for increasing the strength of their developing ability. Their intense concentration on increasing strength to this time has resulted largely in their slighting other aspects of a developing ability which are extremely important. Strength of either a muscle or of a freedom is ineffective unless it is harnessed by and blended with other characteristics such as timing, restraint, coordination with a host of other powers, flexibility, direction, and so on.

In summary, while college students should continue their efforts to secure their hold on the freedom to express themselves, they have a need to recognize that their successes to date have brought with them the more demanding and less easily recognized responsibility to learn how to maintain and artfully use this privilege.

In passing, let us note that there are strong reasons for college students' acting as though their fight to establish individual expression were just beginning rather than nearing a successful completion. Many professors vividly recall the suppressed voice of youth during their own boyhoods and now somewhat anachronistically exhort these collegians militantly to seek the right of expression. As one senior said recently, "When I hear my history professor talk five days a week about the need to further the rights of the individual, I begin to believe that that is the prime cause I need be concerned about." Most college students are alert, as we all need be, to the dangers inherent in the Establishment's (in whatever guise) placing limitations on an individual's right to express himself. Thus firmly convinced of the potential dangers of limitations on individual expression, students are often willing to jump to the conclusion that any limitation on an individual's rights is improper, if not immoral, regardless of who exercises the restriction or for what purpose. There is an even more beguiling reason why so many collegians take the position that the individual's right to expression is the prime, or the only, principle to be established in properly governing relationships between the individual and groups. The use of the individual's right to expression as the *sine qua non* for making all the knotty decisions that arise in individual-group relations provides a seemingly unassailable ethical basis for avoiding many difficult judgments that would otherwise have to be made about such relations. Once one admits that there should be some limitations on individual expression he is faced with making judgments about what these limitations are, when they should be applied, and by whom.

INDIVIDUAL EXPRESSION—RESPONSIBLE OR IRRESPONSIBLE?

Once secured, the right of individual expression, like any other right, can be used responsibly or irresponsibly. If individual expression is to be exercised wisely, it must be applied with judgment and not blindly as an automatic response in all situations. Like muscular power, its effectiveness is diminished when no considerations or principles other than strength are used to guide its application. To the degree that today's collegians continue to enjoy success in their fight for expression, they will find that winning the war to express themselves was easier than maintaining the peace of appropriate application of this right.

Each individual who is capable of doing so has an obligation to speak out in order to help creatively reform society. Without individual expression this essential function cannot be accomplished. This obligation applies to youth as well as to the more mature. When one recognizes that youth can make a constructive contribution to society, the critical question becomes how youth can learn to apply this right constructively, effectively, and in ways which will serve to maintain and enhance it.

Constructive and artful exercise of the right of individual expression involves many considerations. Examination of a few of these considerations will point up the complex learning and judgment-making which are involved in an individual's exercising this right constructively.

BALANCING INDIVIDUAL AND GROUP CONCERNS

One of the first considerations about which an individual must make judgments when expressing himself is whether he should strike a balance between individual and group concerns. On campuses today the most frequent response such an inquiry elicits is that the right of individual expression in inviolable. This position is supported by the idea that, short of barbaric violations of another's rights, an individual is accountable only to himself for his own actions. On the surface these two ideas appear to provide a simple and sensible rationale for resolving all complexities involved in individual and group relations.

However, even a cursory inspection of research accumulated in the field of group dynamics indicates that the individual's functioning has definite and myriad influences on the group's functioning. What the individual does should, to a degree, be governed by the needs of the group because what he does has innumerable consequences for the group as a group and *for the other individuals* in the group as *individuals*. These considerations are illustrated by a recent student meeting which began with useful, orderly, constructive discussion of an issue. The issue was being fully delineated and its several facets adequately explored. After about twenty or thirty minutes the discussion bogged down and meandered, and the group became restless and agitated. In this respect the meeting resembled many meetings of college students today. As the meeting wore on it became apparent why the chairman could not interest the group in keeping the proceedings orderly and in process toward a decision. All the members were so convinced that everyone's right to speak whenever the impulse struck an individual had to be upheld, that no one would attempt to limit repetitious, irrelevant, or exhibitionistic speeches.

What the students apparently did not realize was that by blindly following the principle of granting everyone independent expression, each of them was sacrificing certain of his rights: the right not to have one's time wasted, not to be bored, not to have one's interest in and enthusiasm for his group and its tasks and functions diminished.

MAINTAINING OUR INDIVIDUALITY

Another important consideration in developing mature, constructive, self-expression is the matter of maintaining our individuality when exercising this right. Existentialist writers have made us aware that our individuality is affirmed and strengthened by the simple act of exercising our decision-making power. They have also pointed out that individuality is diminished by unthoughtful adherence to any single principle or opinion. However, as noted above, students often argue that the right to self-expression is the only criterion for determining an individual's relations to other persons or to organizations. Thus, when one argues that individual expression is necessarily the only principle to be followed to govern his relations with his fellows, he forfeits an important decision-making function. Such a one-sided view means that he makes a rote, automatic decision rather than a thoughtful, individually derived decision in selecting among a whole array of principles, tastes, and judgments which have relevance in any given situation. In so doing he ironically loses an important element of his individuality!

BENEFITS THE GROUP PROVIDES

There is another finding from research on groups which suggests a consideration that is pertinent to developing mature self-expression. Such research has uncovered the fact that a group can provide benefits for its members in excess of those derived by merely summing the benefits individuals can provide for themselves. However, to carry on its work and provide these benefits for its individual members, each group or organization must provide for certain group needs, functions, structure, and so forth. If the members of that group concern themselves only with expressing themselves as individuals and not with the group's needs, who will provide for the group needs so that the group can go on providing its unique benefits for its individual members? Research has made it clear that the leader alone cannot provide for all the group functions which must be performed if the group is to continue to provide its special benefits for its individual members.

Opting only for individual expression when one is a member of a group or of an organization—or even of an establishment—may mean the forfeiture of individual expression for some other members of the group. This is not simply the problem that when several people express themselves often and at length there is no time left for others to express themselves. There is, in addition, a more subtle problem. To obtain the constructive contributions (individual expressions) of all its members, a group must establish a climate which is conducive to reasonable expressions of opinion and concern and a climate which insures that all will feel reasonably comfortable in speaking. This climate requires such things as a reasonable degree of order and some form of structure. It requires further that group members take it upon themselves to protect the less forward members from the more forward and to guarantee the opportunity for everyone's view to be given a fair hearing. If loud, aggressive, irrelevant, or self-indulgent expressions dominate a group's functioning, the climate will be such that many individuals will not feel free to express themselves. Group members, as well as the leader, have to contribute to the development of a climate in which all members are given an opportunity to make constructive contributions. Individual judgments about the relevance of each remark are necessary if the group is to move toward its goals, maintain the attention and interest of its members, and have the benefit of its quieter, more reflective members.

MEANINGFUL INDIVIDUALITY

Finally, some argue that individual expression must be nurtured and championed as a means of resisting the depersonalizing forces in modern American life. And so it must. But rigid, rote adherence to individual expression is only a means of depersonalizing independent expression! To be most human, most a person, necessarily involves thought, judgment, and the ability to discern when to submerge one's precious individuality, or right to express it, to the needs of others. One can never have meaningful individuality or the right of expression until he has learned when and where to give it up and when not to use it. The right of individual expression becomes a personalizing force only as each individual makes thoughtful decisions which constructively shape its application and limitations.

10 / Charles W. Havice

CREATIVE CRITICISM AND CAMPUS PROTEST

A critic by definition is a person who tries to look at a matter clearly and objectively, in order to be able to make a fair and well-considered judgment or evaluation about it. We often think of a critic as one who looks primarily for the faults and negative aspects, but he can just as properly be favorable and approving in his judgments. He may or may not *object*, but he should be *objective* in any instance. The principal point is that careful reasoning is involved.

Criticism and ferment are very prevalent on the campus today. (David Mallery aptly entitles his recent study, *Ferment on the Campus.*) Some observers would insist that such conditions are even epidemically prevalent today, an observation we shall later question. Yet criticism is at least as old as Plato's time. In his *Apology*, Plato has his teacher Socrates describe himself as a gadfly—a stinging, biting horsefly, as we would probably put it. This is his statement: "I am a sort of gadfly. The State is a steed who requires to be stirred into life."[1]

THE IMPORTANCE OF THE CRITIC

Any thoughtful person realizes how indispensably important the role of the critic can be. Critics in the world of art and literature,

[1] Benjamin Jowett, *The Dialogues of Plato*, Vol. I (New York, 1920), pp. 413–414.

for instance, exert weighty influence. One thinks of such eminent critics as Olin Downes in music, Walter Kerr in drama, John Ciardi in literature, and Norman Cousins in more general areas. Also, commentators and columnists like Walter Lippmann forcefully demonstrate the power of the critic. Whether we agree or disagree with the point of view expressed by the critic, as intelligent persons we are interested in what he has to say. His dissent, as well as his assent, deserves attention. Dissent is a basic American right!

We must keep in mind, however, that many persons in their very criticisms have been constructive and creative. Henry David Thoreau was uncompromisingly critical in his judgments about the American government. Read again his essay "On the Duty of Civil Disobedience" to realize what a gadfly he was! Many of us today believe he contributed greatly to the true essence of democracy. William Lloyd Garrison was another outspoken critic. He was dragged through the streets of Boston because he condemned slavery. Caring little about his personal safety, he proclaimed: "I will not equivocate, I will not retreat. And I will be heard."[2] Even though now deep in years, Norman Thomas continues vigorously to criticize the elements in our socio-economic life which he believes cause poverty and war. These are but several of the creative critics who have been contributors to society.

Criticism is at times, however, misunderstood. There is a disturbing note about some of the more vocal critics—whether administrators, faculty members, or students. Such critics, more noisy than numerous, accent the carping, cynical, and captious negatives. Such faultfinding ceases logically to be criticism! Criticism, as we have pointed out, is the objective examination which should precede a well-considered evaluation. The critic endeavors to see the situation steadily and see it whole, to paraphrase Matthew Arnold. Arnold further says: "Criticism is a disinterested endeavor to learn and propagate the best that is known and thought in the world."[3] Criticism at its highest level is responsible, rational, and realistic. The columnist Don Marquis once observed that in the name of realism some writers bring all the dead cats from the alley into the parlor and exclaim, "Look, this is America!" Realism, however, insists that

---

[2] William Lloyd Garrison, Salutatory of *The Liberator*, January 1, 1831. See: John Bartlett, *Familiar Quotations* (Boston, 1955), p. 624.

[3] Matthew Arnold, *Essays in Criticism*, No. 1.

the parlor may contain the beauty and fragrance of June roses as well as the ugliness and stench of dead cats. Realism takes into account the whole spectrum of components—the best as well as the worst, and all that lies between—in any life situation. Carping censure and faultfinding therefore distort reality, since they stress only the undesirable and negative elements.

STUDENT ACTIVISM

Closely related to much of the prevalent faultfinding on the American campus are the social phenomena of unrest, protest, rebellion, revolt, vandalism, violence, and other forms of what is being generally labeled today as "student activism." Berkeley has become the generic term for such actions, because that particular campus has received wide publicity. Although it will be indicated later in this discussion that the Berkeley concept is distorted and exaggerated (only three percent of the student body at Berkeley was actively involved), it is nevertheless true that the campus climate currently has more than the normal amount of turbulence. Few campuses can claim today to be ivy-covered, cloistered academes where students are insulated from anything that can disturb the tranquility of the daily routine!

STUDENT INVOLVEMENT IN SOCIAL CHANGE

Dissent and discontent are very much a part of the new posture of contemporary college students—a posture reflecting their serious concerns about many social problems. Although Dean Edmund G. Williamson and John L. Cowan of the University of Minnesota indicate in their study, *The Student and Social Issues*, that apathy, not action, continues to be the common characterisic of the American campus, an increasing number of students are involved in what they regard as relevant and meaningful social change. Race, poverty, and war are central issues which elicit student concerns. Such interests often bring students and faculty members together in a new dimension of sharing and mutual respect. Those of us who have participated in the Selma-Montgomery march and in other overt expressions of social and moral protest have experienced the deep sense of community, faculty and students together, which helps in humanizing the campus. So much for some of the values that inhere in the spirit of dissent and discontent (the latter term in this context being distinguished from malcontent, which is a more chronically negative and rebellious spirit).

MALCONTENTS ARE UNRELIABLE CRITICS

Malcontents can whip up a demonstration on the slightest provocation. They can make mountains out of molehills. They can incite revolts on a moment's notice. They can protest indiscriminately against flimsiest inequities as well as against substantial instances of injustice. Such lack of discrimination, incidentally, lessens the effectiveness of malcontents in coping with legitimate wrongs. Their chronic faultfinding makes them unimpressive and less reliable critics at best. They cry wolf too often.

THE FEW WHO RESORT TO VANDALISM

Vandalism as an overt expression of faultfinding is a serious problem on some campuses. (While vandalism has faultfinding as one of its causative factors, quite obviously faultfinders are not at all automatically suspect of vandalism!) By vandalism, let it be made clear, we are not thinking of the perennial pranks and practical jokes that are relatively less harmful and less costly. Smearing mucilage on the professor's chair is a prank, but defacing a priceless oil painting is vicious vandalism! Property damage and destruction cause incalculable loss to the college. This needless expense likely boomerangs in terms of tuition cost and added fees for the students, but this simple bookkeeping fact apparently goes unrecognized. Some of the loss is irreparable. Expensive furnishings have been mutilated beyond restoration. Long-standing trees on campus have been wantonly damaged. Interior and exterior surfaces of buildings have been senselessly marred beyond refinishing. Often the vandalism causes more personal loss, such as the slashing of convertible tops or the cutting of tires on automobiles left in parking areas. Breaking of locks, windows, vending machines, and classroom and dormitory furniture frequently appears on the vexing list of repairs and replacements. The list is long, much too long.

Why do the grievances, whether real or imagined, and faultfinding of some of the students result in such antisocial activity? The causative factors are too multiple and often too obscure to be accounted for in any simple fashion. One possible explanation is that we live in an affluent society which breeds disregard for property. Another possible explanation is that destructiveness and ruthlessness on campuses merely reflect the same elements which are conspicuous in the troubled and warring world at large. Also, excessive drinking and destructiveness are frequently related. Studies show that vandalism, as well as violence, is often committed by persons who are under the influence of liquor.

Still another possible explanation is more psychological and therefore more subtle: Hostility aggressions are vented irrationally and with no reference to the real situation. One behavioral scientist suggests that too many college students have come from over-permissive homes where few rules or demands were ever imposed. On campus the student for the first time in his life is directly confronted with regulatory principles and authoritarian figures. Since he may feel that he cannot with impunity strike out directly against the administration, the faculty, or even the student governing bodies, his hostility aggression is more deviously aimed against property and possessions that somehow represent those whom he would like to injure or protest against.

Let us consider one further aspect concerning the psychological factors. It is based on the axiom that troubled persons are often destructively aggressive. Psychiatric literature provides many instances of persons who reject themselves, who lack a healthy degree of self-respect and self-acceptance. Such persons tend to transfer this rejection to other persons or to external circumstances. A post-doctoral study was made a few years ago which showed that a great number of persons who were chronic trouble-makers in their communities were unable to accept themselves and were neurotically disturbed individuals. One college dean showed notable insight when a student, responsible for a series of unpleasant problems on the campus, was required to report to the administrator's office. Instead of immediately upbraiding the offender, the dean quietly asked, "Can you tell me why you dislike yourself so much?" That troubled persons are often trouble-makers is an observation which deserves some consideration in our efforts to cope with vandalism. Human behavior is much too complex for us to suppose that, by offering several possible and partial explanations, we thereby have accounted for the disturbing amount of vandalism—that attitude of faultfinding and hostility translated into most senseless and most despicable forms of activity.

We should keep clearly in mind, however, that these extreme expressions of negative criticism represent a very small part of the whole campus community. A clamorous and objectionable minority can often get so much into the limelight that we lose proper focus and perspective. Tabloid headlines often grossly distort and exaggerate the total situation. It should also be borne in mind that in some instances college youths have been blamed for offenses that were actually committed by non-college persons. We overlook the fact that the great majority of students are not chronic faultfinders, and certainly very few are involved in this serious problem of vandalism. At one of the large universities, for example, the dean's office reports that less than a quarter of one percent of the student body became involved in disciplinary action during the past academic year because of destructiveness and related anti-social acts.

SUGGESTIONS FOR HANDLING CRITICISM

To be on the side of constructive criticism and to resist the less mature attitude of carping criticism and faultfinding, the following questions and suggestions may be helpful:

1. *Am I sufficiently informed? Do I have the facts, sufficient facts, for intelligent judgment and action?*

Disraeli once remarked that it is much easier to be critical than to be correct.[4] The instances are many in which a student proceeds to act upon distorted or only partial knowledge. One can expend as much time and effort in tilting quixotically at windmills as in correcting serious wrongs.

Mallery concludes his report, *Ferment on the Campus*, with these perceptive comments: "The colleges are asking a lot of students to expect them to discriminate between real issues and post-adolescent rebellions. Yet they need to ask just this. And from what I heard on these campuses, many students themselves are asking this, and

4 Benjamin Disraeli, in a speech at the House of Commons, January 24, 1860.

are asking it with vigor, and idealism, and dedication that could promise much for our colleges and our nation."[5]

2. *Am I reasonably objective? Do I separate the actual facts from my personal prejudices and subjective involvement?*

We are seldom free from all bias, but we can do our best to evaluate as dispassionately as possible. Truth for truth's sake is the norm which intelligent and mature persons seek to follow, rather than permitting their personal feelings to play too large a role. Carlton J. H. Hayes, one-time Ambassador to Spain, was both an eminent historian and a knighted Catholic layman. In his classic work, *A Political and Social History of Modern Europe*, he discusses the Protestant Reformation with remarkable objectivity. Claude Montefiore, a distinguished Jewish scholar, wrote about the life of Jesus with magnanimous appreciation and notable fair-mindedness. One does not need to sit on the Supreme Court bench to hold to impartial and roundly considered views. The attitude of disinterestedness (but not uninterestedness!) to which Matthew Arnold referred is essential to creative criticism.

3. *Am I a secure and stable enough person to handle criticism, especially unjust criticism, when it is directed toward me? Do I have enough ego strength and self-confidence to handle faultfinding which involves me?*

If much criticism prevails in your immediate environment, do not expect to escape its thrust. You will receive your share! Abraham Lincoln's words are much to the point: "I do the very best I know how; the very best I can; and I mean to keep on doing it to the end. If the end brings me out all right, what is said against me will not amount to anything. If the end brings me out all wrong, then a legion of angels, swearing I was right, will make no difference!"[6]

Lincoln was able to rise above annoying injustices and adverse criticism. He continued to give himself devotedly to an inclusive and ongoing cause. Whether president of the nation, the university, or the business firm, the responsible leader must hold to his well-conceived commitments and convictions in the face of negative criticisms and even condemnations. So must the creative critic. The late

---

[5] David Mallery, *Ferment on the Campus* (New York, 1965), p. 137.
[6] Abraham Lincoln, in a Conversation at the White House, reported by Francis B. Carpenter: *Six Months with Lincoln in the White House* (Watkins Glen, N.Y., 1866).

President John F. Kennedy's book, *Profiles in Courage*, provides dramatic instances of men of conviction who were unswayed by attacks leveled at them. History reminds us that more than one person has managed to turn the potential liability of undeserved faultfinding and adverse criticism into a valuable asset. The Negro leader Booker T. Washington turned the barbs of negative criticism into spears for greater action. He dismissed the belittling critics with the comment, "I will not lower myself to get down into the gutter with any man." His majestic monument at Tuskegee Institute brings to mind the apt verse by Arthur Guiterman:

> "The stones that critics hurl with harsh intent
> A man may use to build his monument."[7]

4. *Am I a part of the problem or a part of the solution?*

A homespun maxim reminds us that those who live in glass houses should not throw stones. A father at a Parent-Teachers Association meeting in a Washington suburb complained about the dishonesty that prevailed in the schoolroom. He pointed out he had given his little daughter a dozen pencils to take to school one morning and that eleven of them were stolen before the day ended. He apparently did not consider it relevant to add that he had appropriated the dozen pencils from the Federal office where he worked! Dr. Harry Emerson Fosdick, a distinguished clergyman, recalls that King Saul publicly denounced witches and then later himself consulted one. He thereby became part of the problem rather than part of the solution. Sitting alone in an automobile that can accommodate four or five passengers, the driver will complain about traffic congestion. The voter will lament the "credibility gap" in the Federal Government but may contribute to the problem by making dishonest tax returns. On campus the student in a variety of ways permits himself to be a part of the very problem against which he is protesting.

5. *Finally, am I sufficiently developed, emotionally and intellectually, to have the capacity to feel grateful?*

Gratitude has been called the mature emotion. Thinking and thanking are both etymologically and psychologically related ("thank" was once in English usage the past tense for "think"). The child

---

[7] Arthur Guiterman, *A Poet's Proverbs*, p. 41. See: Burton Stevenson (ed.) *The Home Book of Quotations* (New York, 1958), p. 339.

thoughtlessly takes; the adult thoughtfully gives. Cardinal Gibbons once remarked that there was not a man in Europe who talked bravely against the church who did not owe it to the church that he could talk at all. The Cardinal's comment applies in some respects to campus situations.

Robert Louis Stevenson once said: "How little we pay our way in life!" The mature student realizes that university life gives far more than one can ever pay for. One can never compensate for the heritage the campus offers in terms of amassed knowledge and cultural opportunities. One can never repay the administrators, trustees, faculty members, and generous benefactors who help make possible an undergraduate education. The perceptive student understands all this and wants to become a contributing part of the on-going community of learners and builders.

THE ROLE OF THE CREATIVE CRITIC

We come now to a consideration which deserves strong emphasis: there is clear evidence that increasing numbers of students have an earnest sense of commitment, concern, and involvement. In the best sense they want to be constructive and creative critics. They have a sensitive awareness that they are part of a society which has weaknesses to be strengthened, wrongs to be righted, and upgrading changes to be effected. They are not content to be spectators; they want to be participants. They deliberately thrust themselves into unpopular and hazardous arenas of social action. Their involvement is often characterized by selflessness and altruism.

Sometimes these constructive critics will change for the better the situation on their local campus. They will create an atmosphere and a set of attitudes that make academic dishonesty among their peers a more reprehensible offense. They will cooperate actively with the administration in insisting upon better housekeeping in the commons, lounge rooms, and other areas where careless litter can be an annoying problem. They will be as alert in speaking out in defense of a maligned faculty member as they are in speaking out against a malingering one! They will come to the support of those seeking excellence. Dr. Nevitt Sanford, distinguished educator and editor of *The American College,* recently said that he believes students still come up to college with a vision of greatness. The creative and constructive critics seem to be unwilling to relinquish that vision!

It is true that some student activism expresses itself, as we have said, in negative and faultfinding forms, but let us further consider the more frequent instances of the constructive commitments and concerns of the students today. In past years, such activism ran the gamut of flagpole sitting, goldfish swallowing, panty raids, and similar stunts. In recent years, let it again be noted that increasing numbers of students have become seriously involved in social, political, and economic issues. To be sure, diverse views stimulate differing activities. Demonstrations both for and against America's involvement in Vietnam exemplify this lack of unanimity. But concerned the students certainly are.

Devoting summer vacations to domestic or foreign projects of social betterment is increasingly taking place. Operation Kindness, now functioning in many of our large cities, is a very down-to-earth project which reaches out to thousands of youngsters who need help and guidance. The Northern Student Movement has assisted countless Negro children and adults. Mental Hospital Companions, Crossroads Africa, and Amigos Anonymus are programs also supported by students. The Lisle Fellowship has a series of projects both at home and abroad. These instances are only several of the many opportunities given the college student for contributing his efforts. Local and special undertakings are also given support. For instance, students will provide leadership in community centers. Students at Oberlin College involved themselves in the special project of rebuilding a wrecked church in the Deep South. Canvassing homes in the South to encourage eligible Negroes to vote is another significant involvement of college students. The Peace Corps and VISTA are notable examples of full-time services given by college youths.

ACCENTING THE AFFIRMATIVE

In concluding this brief discussion of criticism and protest, it should be stressed that on the campus as in any other social situation you will find what you are looking for. Look for faults and weaknesses, and you will find them. Look for affirming, positive, and constructive elements, and you will likewise find them. This presentation emphasizes that, on balance, the latter search is more basically sound and focuses on the more typical and prevalent situations.

The composer Jean Sibelius said that nobody builds a monument to a critic. History gives support to his observation. In workaday language, the wrecking crew at times has its function, but it is the construction gang that more lastingly shows its worth. Accenting the affirmative and concentrating on the constructive can give truer perspective and certainly more satisfaction to most persons. Builders are broader-gauged and more representative college citizens than are belittlers. Creative and constructive criticism, rather than faultfinding and carping criticism, challenges the intellectually and emotionally mature student to greater achievement. He also finds himself in the exhilarating company of many other forward-looking members of the campus community. He rightly belongs to that large company who have not lost, in Professor Sanford's felicitous phrase, "the vision of greatness."

11 / Charles W. Havice

RELIGION ON CAMPUS

When a student leaves his home for college, must he leave his faith in God behind him? One sometimes hears that colleges are hotbeds of heresy, that higher education teaches that all religions are superstitions, and especially that science negates the belief in a Divine Creator.

It is certainly true that religion, perennially a much-discussed topic on any campus, is subject to the ferment and probing that currently pervade the college climate. Complacency, blind faith, and unquestioned compliance are hardly the dominant characteristics of the religious patterns among students today. Students are impatient with the resistance of the religious institution in facing socio-ethical issues like civil rights. Certain aspects of existentialism, ecumenism, demythologizing of religion, and Zen challenge religion in America today.

Foremost among the current challenges, however, is the "God Is Dead" movement. Its impact upon religious thought is of major proportion, and the subject deserves more attention than this passing comment. Although some religious leaders are perturbed about the effects of this new trend, Professor Harvey Cox of Harvard University, author of *The Secular City,* expresses this positive view: "Anyone who thinks the God Is Dead theologians are killing religion in America is one hundred percent wrong. The exact opposite is happening. Religious concern has never been greater than it is today."[1]

Whether one accepts or rejects the above statement made by so authoritative an observer as Harvey Cox, there are evidences that the student does not abandon his religious faith; moreover, there are indications that his college years can clarify and strengthen it. Certainly discussions about religion are flourishing on the contemporary campus. Many students speak knowledgeably about the views of Tillich, Maritain, Buber, Kierkegaard, Bonhoeffer, Bultmann, and others. Religious literacy reaches out far beyond majors in religion or philosophy. Sophisticated and provocative books on religion are being discussed in many sectors of the campus. Cox's aforementioned *The Secular City*, Buber's *I and Thou*, Herberg's *Protestant-Catholic-Jew*, Berton's *The Comfortable Pew*, Earle's *What's Wrong with the Church?*, Robinson's *Honest to God* and *But That I Can't Believe!*, and Friedlander's *Never Trust a God Over 30* are several among many such books.

Rabbi Roland B. Gittelsohn has stated: "One of the most dramatic scenes of increased religious interest is that of our college campuses."[2] Several research projects indicate the religiousness of students. One study, done at Harvard and Radcliffe, reports that of the five hundred students queried seven out of every ten replied affirmatively to the question: "Do you feel that you require some form of religious orientation or belief in order to achieve a fully mature philosophy of life?"[3]

Another study, involving 1,675 undergraduates sampled from ten teachers' colleges, showed that eighty-five percent of these students "felt religion to be an important ingredient for an adequate and satisfying life."[4]

A third study recently conducted at eleven of our great universities involved extensive research on student attitudes and behavior. Nearly three thousand students (exactly 2,975) were asked, among other questions about religion, if they classed themselves as atheists. Out of this sizeable sampling, only one percent of the students said categorically that they were atheists. Since the replies to the question-

---

[1] Will Oursler, "The God-Is-Dead Controversy," *Parade*, May 8, 1966, pp. 14–15.
[2] Roland B. Gittelsohn, *Man's Best Hope* (New York, 1961), p. 4.
[3] Gordon W. Allport, *The Individual and His Religion* (New York, 1956), pp. 36–37.
[4] Rose K. Goldstein, *et al.*, *What College Students Think* (Princeton, N.J., 1960), p. 154.

naires were srictly anonymous, likely they were honestly given. In this same important study, three-fourths of the students said they believed in God, and nearly half (48%) of them selected the following statement as most accurately describing their ideas about Deity: "I believe in a Divine God, creator of the universe, who knows my innermost thoughts and feelings and to Whom one day I shall be accountable."[5] Because this research was done by experts and involved outstanding institutions, these responses are most impressive.

The above studies are consistent with historical considerations. Almost all of the leading and long-established colleges in this country, as well as those in Europe, were founded by religious organizations; moreover, they were usually instituted for religious purposes, such as the training of the clergy. Of course, there are many colleges in America today that are not officially related to any religious denomination, but even these institutions are often influenced by religious factors. Later in our discussion, we shall show that religious influences and activities are actually very evident on the American campus.

One such influence is directly attributable to the fact that religious beliefs are generally held by the students themselves. Many come from religious homes. After all, the focal fact about the American way of life is that it has been built on religious foundations. Our American democracy at its best represents Judaeo-Christian ideals put into action. As Americans, we want the Church separated from the State, but we do not want to separate God from government. From the days of our founding fathers, we have declared that we look to God for guidance. ". . . One nation, under God" we affirm. American homes are consequently a part of our religious heritage. Most babies and children are baptized or confirmed in the religious faith of the household. Most Americans are married by a minister, priest, or rabbi. Most persons are buried with the last rites of their denomination.

It is therefore understandable that students bring to college many of the beliefs and religious influences of their home. Like Thomas Carlyle, they will acknowledge that they stand on the sunken pillars of the faith of their mothers and fathers. In a reflective moment, a student recently asserted that the most prized influence in his life was the godly example set by his parents. The brothers

[5] *Ibid.*

Arthur H. Compton and Karl T. Compton, both great scientists, on repeated occasions spoke of the great debt they owed to their parents for the religious training they received from them and upon which they developed their own faith. The present writer, having taught many advanced courses in religion, can recall numerous instances where students indicated that their understanding of basic principles of belief was gained from the experiences and knowledge they had acquired at home. Obviously, a student does not at the moment of entering college break off all the experiences he has accumulated throughout his formative years.

THE URGE TO GROW

While keeping in mind the facts we have just discussed, we must nevertheless deal with another significant observation. The college student early in his first year finds that he is encountering many new and sometimes conflicting ideas. Likely a student would not decide to go to college at all if he had no interest in tackling new ideas, dealing with more complex views, coping with varied and controversial opinions, and thereby maturing in his thoughts, feelings, and beliefs. He expects to have his intellectual muscles stretched by what he learns in the classroom, library, and laboratory. He wants to grow, to have his mental horizons expanded, remembering the truth in the old adage that "the horizon broadens as we climb." He realizes that growing up, whether physically or mentally, can at times be awkward, challenging, and difficult. But grow up he must! He must mature in his religious understanding, too. Even Saint Paul had this experience. He said: "When I was a child, I spoke as a child, I understood as a child, I thought as a child: but when I became a man, I put away childish things." (I Corinthians 13:11)

In connection with this urge to grow and mature, two helpful observations are suggested at this point. Bear in mind that the college student as an educated person must sometimes take the responsibility and exercise the right to use his own trained mind, to rely on his own powers of reasoning, and especially to stand by his own value judgments and convictions. When and when not to do this is, of course, a difficult decision to make; no easy generalization can be given here. Let us cite a few simple instances, however, when it becomes obvious that the student should feel free independently to accept or reject: He may not like the sports, the hobbies, the foods, the plays, the music or the leisure-time books that even his most learned professor enthusiastically enjoys. The fact that his most distinguished teacher of history endorses a particular make of automobile does not in the slightest dissuade the student from regarding that make with strong disapproval.

In light of the above situations, the college student guards against the fallacy of assuming that expertness in one field guarantees expertness in a quite unrelated field. Will Rogers made a point: "There is nothing so stupid as the educated man, if you get off the subject he was educated in." Henry Ford was acknowledged the world over as a pioneering expert in the automotive industry, but when he conceived the notion of sending his "Peace Ship" to other nations, his judgment was anything but expert. Thomas A. Edison was a world-famed inventor, but when he gave his critical views about higher education at a noted institution of learning, he made statements that even a schoolboy would find ridiculous. William Jennings Bryan was a statesman of great integrity and idealism. But the historian Charles A. Beard significantly said of Bryan that he never developed beyond the age of twelve in his religious thinking. The point is, occasionally a college student will hear or read a statement about religion made by an authority or expert in such a field as psychology or biology or anthropology. Yet is that authority competent to give information or make judgments about faith in God, the value of prayer, or any other principal aspect of religious belief and truth? He may or may not be thus qualified. The discerning student will do some careful thinking on his own part.

The second observation that can be helpful to the student who wants to grow religiously concerns the place of doubt in his thinking. Doubt should not be regarded as a barrier that prevents one from gaining new insight and greater truth, but as a bridge which carries one from a limited to a fuller understanding. Doubt has often provided the impetus to achieving greater heights of truth. This impetus is illustrated repeatedly in both scientific and religious fields. Lord Tennyson's familiar observation applies to the value of doubt in the latter field: "There lives more faith in honest doubt, believe me, than in half the creeds."[6] Carefully considered doubt is a friend and not a foe of mature religious faith.

[6] Lord Alfred Tennyson, "In Memoriam," XCVI, Stanza 3.

FAITH AND REASON

In developing his own convictions after reckoning with the above-stated encounters, the student will need to consider a profound truth about religion. Simply stated, it is this: Religion is not unreasonable, but neither is it merely reason. It is also faith. The centuries-old argument has been whether religion should be based on knowledge or on faith. Today, like the outmoded argument as to whether heredity or environment makes us what we are, we no longer think in terms of either-or but in terms of both-and. Saint Anselm's motto is to be recommended: "I believe in order that I may know." Often in our daily lives we go as far as knowledge or reason can carry us, and then we take the leap of faith. William James, one of America's greatest teachers, said in his "Will to Believe" that faith in the fact can help create the fact.[7] The truth of his observation can be seen in our daily experiences. If men had waited to know all about electricity before they were willing to make use of it, candles and oil lamps would still be the sources of our illumination!

Because simple faith is an indispensable element in religion, the college student will be reminded of what may well be true of the influences in his home life. In some instances, his parents may not have had extensive training in logic and scientific analysis. However adequate their education, it may not have been in scientific fields. They may nevertheless have gained a deep religious understanding and faith, which can give to life an inner peace and joy to be envied by even the most sophisticated scholar. Pascal said, "The heart has its reasons which reason itself does not know."[8] If a student should be faced with the dilemma of having to accept anti-religious arguments in the classrooms—it happens—and thereby having to abandon a principle of faith very meaningful to him, he will do well to recall Pascal's words.

We have been discussing the facts that colleges are favorable rather than hostile to religion, that the student will find the religious influences of his home have continuing value for him, that increased knowledge need not decrease his religious faith, and that college encourages growth and maturity. There is an amalgam that holds these facts together and helps to make any discussion of one's faith more

[7] William James, *The Will to Believe and Other Essays in Popular Philosophy* (New York, 1896), p. 251.
[8] Blaise Pascal, *Pensées*, Sect. IV, No. 277.

coherent in all its aspects. It is that one's faith, in last analysis, has to be one's own. A person can be surrounded by expert swimmers, he can listen carefully to all their experiences and instruction, and he can inherit leather-bound books on the art and science of swimming. But only *he* can swim for himself.

This example is analogous to one's faith. It must be internalized, to use a term popular among psychologists. One's religion is not a bequest. It is a conquest. The student at college, if he is to grow religiously, must do his own growing. Since we have already admitted that growth presents difficulties, let us now consider at least one specific challenge which the student will encounter in his quest for religious maturity.

This challenge derives from the fact that colleges reflect the scientific and technological era of which we today are so much more a part than were our grandparents. Unless a student thinks logically and clearly, he may decide that science is in conflict with religion. He may forget that courses in science are often taught in colleges that are directly controlled by religious denominations. Astronomy is taught at Southern Methodist University, biology at Brandeis University, chemistry at Catholic University, psychology at the Episcopal Theological School, physics at Holy Cross College. And so it goes.

Furthermore, many of the leading scientists are men and women of religious faith who are active in their denominational groups. Several years before his death, the Nobel prize-winning physicist, Robert A. Millikan, stated that he could see no conflict between his scientific knowledge and his religious faith. Relative to the same point, a chemist and dean of the graduate school at a large university recently wrote to the author as follows:

Faith and religion can be a source of strength to any thinking person in facing the pressures of life today. There is no conflict between religion and science; the more one knows of science, the more one should feel the need for a religion to govern behavior in terms of great moral principles.[9]

Another outstanding scientist and head of a large physics department also wrote to this author:

I have been teaching and carrying on research in mathematics and physics for thirty years. I have never found science to be incompatible with an intelligent approach to religion. In fact, the more I learn of the

[9] Dean Arthur A. Vernon, Northeastern University.

beautiful and vast amount of order present in the various systems comprising the universe, the more I become convinced that a Supreme Intelligence is the only answer.[10]

Having had the opportunity during the past several years to visit over sixty colleges, this writer can cite an impressive number of instances at these institutions of higher learning where some of the most active participants in the religious life are scholars and scientists of national distinction.

We have already emphasized that education means growth. This emphasis can be applied with special force as we deal with the question of relating scientific knowledge to religion. Scientific knowledge has developed with unprecedented rapidity in recent years. Who would attempt to argue that a high school course in physics qualifies that student for membership on a team of nuclear physicists! The knowledge gained from that one elementary course may not be false, but it is obviously inadequate. Similarly, religious knowledge (not faith!) brought from home to college certainly may not be false, but again, it may be inadequate—at least in coping with the challenges sometimes encountered in advanced courses at college. A distinguished British thinker of our time, Dr. John B. Phillips, has entitled one of his books *Your God Is Too Small*. In it he describes such immature views of God as "Resident Policeman," "Parental Hangover," "God-in-a-Box," and "Second-Hand God."[11]

Such views remind one of the villager who said, "When I think of God, I think of a big oblong blur"; or of the boy who pictured God as a vague composite of Father Time, Moses, and the Grim Reaper; or of the man who described God as a vengeful, vindictive god of wrath (as some isolated statements in the Bible admittedly do suggest) and received this comment from a more thoughtful man: "Your description of God is my description of the devil."

Now, of course, none of us is able satisfactorily to describe God, else He would no longer be God. A view of Him that is small enough for our understanding would not be large enough for our needs. Yet in this rapidly growing age of science, we need to enlarge our personal conceptions of the God who can be viewed as the Creator of all science and truth.

---

[10] Professor Reginald G. Lacount, Northeastern University.
[11] John B. Phillips, *Your God Is Too Small* (New York, 1953), pp. 15–18.

Dr. Henry N. Russell, noted astronomer at Princeton University, gave a lecture on the various galaxies—the Milky Way especially—with its hundreds of millions of stars. Then he said, "Our world is infinitesimal in comparison." A woman in the audience later asked him, "If our world is so little and the universe is so great, can we believe God pays any attention to us?" Professor Russell's reply is one worth remembering. He said, "That depends upon how great a God you believe in!"[12]

Sam Walter Foss has put the same truth in a poem which in the following stanza describes a boy's increasing view of God:

> As wider skies broke on his view,
>   God greatened in his growing mind;
> Each year he dreamed his God anew,
>   And left his older God behind.

RELIGIOUS PROGRAMS AND RESOURCES ON CAMPUS

At the beginning of this discussion it was indicated that there is evidence that colleges have serious religious concerns. Let us now take a more careful look at the American campus. What forms do these religious interests take? What religious activities are to be found at college? In short, in what ways can the student coming to college expect to find support and encouragement for his own religious development?

In the first place, at the majority of colleges today the student will find a group of fellow students who belong to his own denomination. If he goes to a denominational college, the number of students belonging to that particular denomination will often, but not always, be in the majority. In such instance, his feeling of belonging, which is an important contribution that religion makes, will be easily satisfied. If the student goes to a nonsectarian institution, he will nevertheless find a like-minded religious group.

Most large institutions have an impressive variety of denominational organizations. The Baptist Club, the B'nai B'rith Hillel, the Canterbury Club, the Christian Science Organization, the Eastern Orthodox Club, the Lutheran Club, the Newman Club, the United Christian Fellowship and the Wesley Foundation are typical groups.

[12] *Dictionary of American Biography* (New York City, 1932), Vol. V, p. 216.

At a few of the largest institutions, the number of such clubs reaches twenty or more. Usually an interfaith council enables the groups to unite in many common endeavors. Incidentally, one of the advantages of being on a campus where there are numerous religious groups is that one can exchange points of view and learn to appreciate beliefs different from one's own. It usually works out that a student tries to learn more about his own denomination when he has opportunities to participate in discussions which cross sectarian lines. Most important, he probably comes to understand more fully, as Emerson stated, that "the things that unite us are ever finer than the things that divide us."

A second source of encouragement to a student's religious growth is the regularly held chapel services that are to be found on most campuses today. Sometimes these services are very similar in form and content to the worship services which the student attended at home. Sometimes they are not. In either instance, the services can provide valuable moments of instruction and inspiration to those who will take advantage of the opportunities to attend. Some of the more relevant sermons delivered in the college chapel can be long-remembered contributions to one's religious understanding.

A third source of encouragement to a student's religious growth is closely related to the one just previously mentioned. Where there is a chapel, probably there is a chaplain, or a group of denominational chaplains, or a dean of chapel. Even where there is no chapel, there may be chaplains. One of the evidences of the increased interest taken by colleges in the religious maturing of students is the marked growth in the number of chaplains and deans of chapel appointed on campuses. The membership of the National Association of College and University Chaplains and Directors of Religious Life, as well as that of the National Campus Ministry Association and the Association for the Coordination of University Religious Affairs, has shown steady increase in recent years. These chaplains and deans have had special professional training for the responsibilities they assume in dealing with all aspects of religious life on the campus. Most of all, they are well qualified to give individual counsel and support when the student needs spiritual help. These religious leaders frequently assist in organizing informal group discussions dealing with moral and religious problems.

A fourth source of encouragement to a student's religious growth is the credit-giving courses in religion offered on most campuses. Not only are more institutions giving such courses, but a larger variety of such courses is being offered. Typical of such offerings are The History of Religion, Comparative Religions, The Philosophy of Religion, The Religions of America, and Contemporary Religious Trends.

A fifth source is afforded by the excellent opportunity at college to read the many available books and magazines on religion to be found in the library. Even a relatively small library will provide a variety of literature on religion, since the subject is one of pervasive interest among educated persons. Of special value are the magazines and periodicals that represent many religious viewpoints, both within and between denominational groups. *The Christian Century, Commentary, Commonweal, Christianity and Crisis, Religious Education, The Journal for the Scientific Study of Religion*, and *The Journal of Bible and Religion* are typical journals.

A sixth source is the coffee house sponsored by religious organizations. Students gather in an informal and relaxed setting to discuss over coffee cups their issues of concern. Along with folk music and other programs, the subjects of politics, social betterment, drama, college life, ethics, and religion are freely explored. Often a clergyman is invited to participate in the discussions and to serve as a resource person. Sometimes the coffee house is nominally under the auspices of one particular religious denomination; more often, it is interfaith and ecumenical in support. Openness and freedom from institutionalism are dominant features of this popular venture.

A final source of encouragement to a student's religious growth is probably the most effective of all. It is simply the day-to-day companionship with persons whose spiritual strength and idealism exert a profound influence in a quiet but powerful way. Religion is caught more than it is taught. Living in the presence of the best is more likely to be true in college years than at any other period in one's life. Devoted and dedicated teachers—and they are in the majority —by example more than by precept will often demonstrate that reverence for God, respect and compassion for fellowman, belief in the good and true and beautiful, and high ethical ideals are convincing evidences of their mature religious development. In such company, comprising not only teachers but many fellow students as well, the individual student can find powerful incentives to grow in faith and knowledge of God. At its best, college offers all this and more.

While this discussion about the student and his faith is brief and incomplete, it nevertheless attempts to deal with the one most important consideration in anyone's life. When Daniel Webster was asked what for him was the greatest concern, he replied that his greatest concern was his ultimate accountability to his Maker. Who could disagree with Webster on that point? Religion is an intensely personal matter, a truth we recognized in an earlier part of this chapter. H. G. Wells, in his novel *Mr. Britling Sees It Through*, gives pointedness to this truth in the words of his principal character:

Religion is the first thing and the last thing, and until a man has found God and has been found by God, he begins at no beginning, he works to no end. He may have his friendships, his partial loyalties, his scraps of honour. But all these things fall into place and life falls into place only with God. Only with God.[13]

Yet, as deeply personal as religion is, no college student in the complex world of today would be satisfied to hold only this single view. He is very much aware that there is another basic dimension to religion: its social applications, its ethical implications in a world of persons, its moral principles involving all aspects of human society. Several recent studies of campus life show that those students who are highest on the religiousness scale (that is, who are most actively committed to their religion) are usually highest in their moral standards and attitudes in reference to drink, sex, cheating, and the other moral issues. In a national study of campus morality in which the writer is currently involved, there are already many evidences in the preliminary findings that the religious factor is an influential one in promoting moral behavior.

The social impact of religion as the foundation for ethics extends beyond the campus; it permeates all phases of modern society. All great issues confronting the world today are moral considerations fundamentally. The problems of racial injustice, political corruption, poverty, crime and war are not basically political or social or economic problems. They are basically moral problems. In our Judaeo-Christian tradition morality is strongly rooted in religion. It is therefore understandable that we regard religion as being relevant in solving man's social ills.

On the positive side, religion is often the dominant motivating

[13] H. G. Wells, *Mr. Britling Sees It Through* (New York, 1917), p. 442.

force behind student participation in many forms of constructive social action. The campus religious organizations are providing from their membership volunteers for helping the underprivileged both at home and abroad. Typical instances involving religiously and ethically motivated students are Americanization classes, work with troubled children, civil rights programs, the Peace Corps, reading to the blind, and special foreign projects—like the Lisle Fellowship program with headquarters at the University of Michigan. In many ways the impact upon the community made by religiously concerned students is one of the most encouraging aspects of American life today. Any person who has the opportunity to observe the vitality of this student concern can convincingly attest to this fact and provide many supporting examples.

A frequently quoted statement of Alfred North Whitehead is appropriate here. This distinguished philosopher said, "Moral education is impossible apart from the habitual vision of greatness." The heritage and hope of America are in its moral and ethical education. In our Judaeo-Christian culture, we look most of all to our religious faith for that vision of greatness. The religious challenge confronting our nation today has incalculable social consequences. At the same time it has profoundly personal implications. Americans believe that one lone individual can exert immeasurable influence. Especially in moral integrity and religious idealism does the contribution of one person count significantly. You will recall the way Edward Everett Hale put this truth:

> I am only one
> But still I am one.
> I cannot do everything
> But still I can do something;
> And because I cannot do everything
> I will not refuse to do the something
> I can do.[14]

[14] Edward Everett Hale, For the *Lend-A-Hand Society*. See: John Bartlett, *Familiar Quotations* (Boston, 1955), p. 624.

APPENDIXES

I | Joy D. Winkie

RESPONSIBILITY AND

COOPERATIVE EDUCATION

The ivory-tower sanctity of the college campus has been swept into virtual oblivion by the flood of applicants clamoring for admittance at the gates of higher education. Urban universities have the same plight as the old woman who lived in a shoe and had so many children she didn't know what to do. All too frequently, the result has been a somewhat less than harmonious cohabitation of collegians and local citizens. The latter are unaccustomed to the casual manners, the liberal views, and the exuberance of campus life. The collegians on their part resent the unacademic atmosphere of the subway and the asphalt jungle.

But in addition to the material intrusion of one culture upon another, there has been a mental intrusion which, in many instances, has been of far greater consequence. The academic scientist has become the industrial consultant and the campus sociologist, the architect of urban renewal. The college president fights a never-ending battle for tax-free land in cities eager for new revenue. The student, once secure in his ivory tower, is now thrust into daily contact with the harsh realities of everyday life.

In some institutions this culture shock has been far less traumatic than in others. Since the turn of the century, a number of universities, through adoption of the Cooperative Plan of Education, have sought to polish and perfect the relationship between academic theory and practice. Although the student at this type of institution may not enjoy the comparative leisure of the traditional campus, he emerges from the college experience better prepared to meet the demands of the workaday world. In the course of his education, the "co-op" student often is required to make decisions involving personal and professional responsibility and integrity which do not confront the average student until after graduation and the beginning of a career. The co-op student's relationship to the university and to his cooperative employer is totally different from that of a student enrolled in a conventional curriculum and independently engaged in part-time employment. The university and the employer, in turn, have a totally different relationship with the co-op student.

THE STUDENT'S RESPONSIBILITY TO THE UNIVERSITY

Since it is the university and not the student which places him in a company's employ, and thereby assumes responsibility for his conduct, the student is viewed as a representative of the university during his cooperative work assignments. A poor co-op student, therefore, can ruin another student's opportunity for employment or advancement, inasmuch as companies frequently find fault with the "Co-op Plan" rather than with the individual. If the university is staking its reputation on every student it sends out for employment, the student has a responsibility to the university to perform his duties in a creditable manner. Most students are perfectly capable of doing so, but there are some who, if left to their own devices, would be virtually unemployable. Some schools take the position that the cooperative program should be restricted to the better students only. Others argue that so long as a student is progressing, he should have the opportunity of benefiting from the cooperative experience. Many employers generously agree to take on students of lesser ability knowing that such students constitute a minority and do not seriously affect the company's high opinion of the cooperative system. This fact goes unacknowledged by many students. Some students, on the other hand, readily admit that they, as employers, would not be anxious to put certain of their classmates in positions involving any degree of responsibility.

Students sometimes fail to recognize that *they* are transient, whereas the universities and companies involved *are not*. At times, certain rules may seem contrary to an individual student's interest; yet the long-range objectives of the program may require establishment of these rules. The student who becomes more concerned with "bucking the system" than doing the best job possible may do irreparable damage to the system and to the educational opportunities of classes yet to come. Youth's desire to challenge the status quo needs to be tempered, and the cooperative work periods often provide an opportunity to "come of age" in this respect. Employers resent having a "fresh young kid" tell them how to run their business, but they are more likely to humor a co-op student than an employee fresh out of college. Nevertheless, the earlier in life this lesson is learned, the better the chances for a student's harmonious adjustment to the realities of the workaday world. This is not to imply that employers are not open to suggestion, but students must learn to distinguish between suggestion and impertinence!

THE UNIVERSITY'S RESPONSIBILITY TO THE STUDENT

The university's responsibilities under the Cooperative Plan are clearly defined. Students who enroll in a cooperative school do so with the expectation that the education they receive will have an added dimension not found in a conventional college. A university makes this promise in its promotional literature and therefore has a moral obligation to "deliver the goods." If the job experience does not contribute to the educational growth of the student, the university has failed in its commitment just as much as the student who fails to live up to his obligations during a cooperative assignment.

Although, as was mentioned previously, the university has a responsibility to insure the perpetuation of "the system," as an institution of higher learning, it has an even greater responsibility to insure the growth of the individual. The old adage that rules are made to be broken is perhaps nowhere more true than in education, where the search for a new way, a new approach, or a new bit of knowledge is fundamental.

There will be times when the cooperative work interests of the student may seem to be opposed to those of the university. For instance, a student may wish to change jobs for some reason. The coordinator, knowing that there have been a series of job changes or other problems with this same employer recently, may feel that this particular student's departure could prove to be the straw that broke the camel's back, with the result that the company might withdraw from the program completely. If the jobs are generally good, it would be in the university's best interests to maintain the company relationship; and the coordinator may urge the student to remain one more term until the change can be made without jeopardizing the entire program. The final decision as to whether or not the student leaves the company rests with the student and his coordinator. The student should not be asked to continue beyond one additional term, however, even if it were to mean loss of the company as a cooperative employer.

THE STUDENT'S RESPONSIBILITY TO THE COMPANY

When I came here, I guess like most high school seniors, I was looking for a high-paying job which would enable me to earn enough to cover my first year's tuition. During the summer I worked for $95 a week at . . . Company in a storeroom. After 35 weeks of college training, I made $40 a week as a messenger boy down in the financial district. I'm not saying that I minded taking the job, but when you get your pay check cut in half after 35 weeks of college training, you wonder what will happen when you get to be a college senior.

The above student comment indicates an immature understanding of the purpose of the Cooperative Plan and the role of the co-op student. The student's use of the term "college training" suggests a vocational rather than an educational orientation toward college and an exaggerated idea of what a freshman in college is worth to business. Unlike a skilled laborer, a student cannot expect his pay to be in proportion to the amount of time he puts into what he considers specialized training. The freshman-year courses, designed as they are to give a broad introduction to a variety of subjects, "train" a student for no specific skill. This is not and never has been their purpose.

Employment in a storeroom more than likely was more dependent on brawn than brain. The student in question had enough of the former to warrant $95 a week, but not enough of the latter in a field like finance to warrant equal compensation. The salary itself is never the total picture, for it is based on the student's contribution where he is employed. First- or second-year nonscience liberal arts majors have very little to contribute to the operation of a company, whereas a first- or second-year engineer may already have the skills of a low-level technician. Therefore, the engineering student's salary will be appreciably higher than that of the "unskilled" liberal arts student, who has no skill to offer an employer, with the possible exception of typing and shorthand. (Even these skills are frequently lacking as many high school students enrolled in a college preparatory curriculum think it beneath their dignity to take typing, shorthand, or other so-called "commercial" courses.) *A student needs to recognize the fact that every employer is spending money and time training him, even if he at the same time feels that he is providing "cheap labor."*

The need for humility about their abilities and potential use to an employer has been the subject of many student discussions, out of which have come eight unofficial guidelines which the students themselves feel it important to follow during the early stages of their cooperative work experience:

1. Be humble during a job interview. Most employers prefer humility to cockiness. (In this instance the students cited a case in which the boy who was overconfident of his capabilities, and did not hesitate to show this, lost out to a second boy who was less sure of himself but "willing to learn.")

2. Always start a job with an open mind. Preconcieved notions of what a job should or should not be can prevent you from getting the most out of a situation.

3. Take it easy at the beginning of a new job—feel your way and follow directions. Don't feel compelled to act as though you knew it all.

4. Don't expect to tell an employer how to run his business. Do your own job well and he may subsequently ask your opinion.

5. Don't expect a rug on the floor, three phones, and a private secretary!

6. When you meet "complainers" at work and at school, take a close look at their abilities. The loudest are many times those with the least ability.

7. Be willing to accept the small routine job graciously and you

will earn the better job next time. People will respect and appreciate someone who is willing to "pitch in" more than the individual who complains of a job being beneath his educational level.

8. Try to learn something from every cooperative assignment, even when its educational value is not immediately apparent.

This final point was discussed in great detail by one group of students interviewed. They agreed that even the job of office boy or mail boy can be valuable if a student is willing to learn from the experience. One boy put it this way:

A seldom appreciated advantage that accrues to the cooperative education graduate is the opportunity to work at a variety of levels with people of a variety of abilities. The average college graduate has no concept of the problems of the factory worker, but the co-op who has worked alongside such an individual understands his views and values. The best way to learn to communicate with people is to work with them at their level. It won't hurt you. You may not like it. You may even hate it, but there are many benefits to be gained from the association.

If it does nothing else, boredom with an unchallenging job can motivate a student to want more in life and make him more willing to work for it, when firsthand experience shows him the alternative.

In addition to this responsibility to give generously and graciously of one's time and effort, a co-op student also has an obligation to respect and be willing to learn from the older employees of the company. Although there may be times when a student's ideas and those of his supervisor differ, the latter's years of experience are generally worth far more than the textbook knowledge of the student who has never had to consider the time or cost which might be involved in implementing a new system.

A student also has the obligation of maintaining proper business decorum in an office environment. Flirting with the secretaries, "horsing around with the boys," or being preoccupied with one's own personal appearance is definitely out of place. Employers seldom like to hire a girl with an extreme hairstyle for fear she will spend half her day in the powder room trying to keep it intact; or a boy with a suave "man-about-town" manner who they fear might be more interested in making time with the secretaries than doing his job. A student also has a responsibility to dress appropriately on his cooperative work assignment. Although generally advisable, suits for boys and dresses for girls are not an iron-clad rule, for there are times when the nature of the work dictates the attire. One rather humorous example of this was provided by a young lady who appeared for her first day of work at the National Archives in Washington, D.C., dressed in a lovely wool sheath and high heels, only to find this costume completely inappropriate to the occasion.

I was always told not to dress in a collegiate manner when I was on co-op—no pleated skirts or sweaters, but dresses or skirts and blouses instead. When I went to work the first day, I was wearing heels and a dress. They took one look at me and said, 'Well, you can go home and change or you can work barefoot.' I had library ladders to climb and the boxes of records were caked with dust. The job was interesting, but as for 'proper dress' . . . !

In matters of dress, it is once again important for students to remember that they represent not only themselves, but their university, and this realization coupled with common sense should dictate their mode of attire.

Finally, a student has an ethical responsibility to an employer which stipulates that loyalty to one's employer for as long as the employer-employee relationship exists is an absolute necessity and a fundamental part of the cooperative work agreement. Loyalty to one's employer and honesty in one's relationship with him are very important traits in the professional world. A graduating senior who possesses no sense of professional responsibility is a poor risk to any employer regardless of his academic or practical know-how. As a representative of his university, a student acting unethically can do great harm to the institution itself, as the following case history emphasizes:

In the winter of his final year, a graduating senior accepted a university's offer of a graduate assistantship to begin the following September. When he subsequently received a second offer more to his liking, he accepted it but failed to notify the original university until the opening of the academic year that he would not be joining their staff in September. The "jilted" Chairman of the Department, faced with a staff shortage and an unused stipend, wrote to the student requesting an explanation for his action but received no reply. In October, he wrote again, but still there was no reply.

Finally, on November 19, he wrote the following letter to the student's undergraduate Department Chairman. The second paragraph is of particular note.

Dear Professor . . . ,

Mr. . . . , a graduate of your Department of last spring, applied for admission to our Graduate School, and was admitted and offered an assistantship on the strength of his academic record and the recommendations we received from you, Professor . . . , and Professor. . . . He sent his written acceptance of the offer in late February. He wrote on August 20 stating he did not wish a reservation for dormitory housing and acknowledging my request that he report on September 11. On September 11, I received a letter informing me of his "withdrawal" as a graduate student. I am enclosing a copy of that letter as well as copies of letters I wrote him on September 11 and again on October 16. No response has been received to either of these two letters, and I must admit that that fact causes me to doubt strongly that Mr. . . .'s last minute withdrawal was caused by circumstances of bona fide seriousness.

In communicating all of this to you, it is not my purpose to pursue Mr. . . . any further or to cause him any difficulty whatsoever. It occurs to me that the information may be of value to you and your colleagues, however. Your recommendations were uniformly strong in this instance and surely all of you have been severely let down. On our part, the experience probably cannot avoid influencing future deliberations of the Admissions Committee concerning applications from your Department. I am aware that that may be totally unjust, but since the number of available supporting stipends is limited, we will of course prefer not to take risks, all other things being equal. In view of all these factors, I thought it best to communicate with you straightforwardly on the subject. I feel confident that this was a wholly isolated instance, but at the same time perhaps all of us need to do more than we have been doing to impress upon our seniors the seriousness of their professional obligations, and the fact that immature actions on their part can reflect much more widely than upon themselves alone.

Sincerely yours,
(Signature)
Chairman

THE COMPANY'S RESPONSIBILITY TO THE STUDENT

There are few people who will deny that business and industry need the talents and respect of young people if our society is to continue to enjoy the high standard of living to which we have become accustomed. This being the case, business and professional employers must live up to the responsibilities they have voluntarily assumed through their stated interest in participating in the Cooperative Plan. Students who are exposed to unethical practices in business at an age when they are striving to determine the best way to get ahead, cannot help being tempted to take shortcuts if this appears to be an accepted form of company behavior. Students are quick to discern the phoney, and a company which subscribes to one policy on paper and another in practice will be readily spotted by a co-op student. Rightly or wrongly, many businesses and professions have attained reputations for unethical practices which will be changed only when the public is assured that the policies of the past are no longer acceptable.

Co-op students are exposed to these practices at an earlier age than the four-year college graduate, and they frequently tell of observing instances of "cheating" ranging from employees sleeping in stockroom, to petty theft of office supplies, to elongated coffee breaks and lunch hours, to padding of expense accounts. Observation of, or occasional forced participation in such behavior is not what is meant by gaining "practical" as opposed to theoretical knowledge through cooperative employment! Some students have been asked to falsify reports while on a cooperative assignment. A student is in an extremely difficult position if he knows that refusal to do so may mean the loss of his job. And what is a coed to do when her employer is making advances? Report it, embarrass her employer and lose her job, or remain silent and attempt to handle the problem alone? This is highly unfair to a student, whose college degree is dependent upon the successful completion of cooperative work assignments. Political science majors have been known to lose excellent jobs to party hacks hired in the wake of a change in political administration. One might argue that this is part of the American political tradition and any student contemplating a political career had best learn this early in the game, but such a callous excuse for unethical behavior seems totally out of place in an educational program. Furthermore, it is just this type of experience that discourages students from entering the field of politics, where there can be no question as to the need for honest and dedicated personnel.

Students also are quick to discern inconsistencies in a company's hiring policies regarding race, religion, or nationality. Students finding that they cannot have a given job because of their religion, nationality, or color, may become very cynical about the very profession to which they aspire. This too is *not* a goal of Cooperative Education, and it is the employer's responsibility to insure that it does not become a by-product of the Cooperative Plan.

Questions also have been raised as to the company's attitudes toward its co-op employees. Students are individuals with names and identities, talents and weaknesses, deserving of an employer's time, recognition, and respect. To call a student "Co-op" in place of his given name is inexcusable, but it has been known to happen on more than one occasion. In addition, there also have been reports of companies' failing to inform students that their services were no longer desired, simply because the employers did not want the task of giving the students bad news. It is not fair for the university to have to assume this unpleasant task, particularly when the students have been led to believe that they were well liked and that their work was satisfactory. If employers want the pleasure of informing students of their raises and promotions, they must also assume the responsibility of telling them when their performance, appearance, or behavior is not acceptable. The companies' interest in maintaining a good surface image at the expense of the individual students is as incompatible with the purpose of co-op as the above-mentioned breaches of etiquette and professional ethics.

Although these unethical realities in life are hard for students to face, they many times are made easier by the "in and out" nature of the Cooperative Plan. The classroom provides an often needed buffer between the periods of cooperative employment which may expose students to disillusionment. A degree of maturity and understanding of the ways of the world are an important part of the college years, but they should never be permitted to rob the student of his inalienable right to be a carefree collegian during at least part of his college career!

It is a sad commentary on our society when professors of business administration report that "students seem to think there is very little difference between smart tactics and legal tactics when it comes to a company's abuse of a law or an antitrust decision." What these students observe on co-op can either repudiate or substantiate their beliefs. Should it be the latter, there can be little hope for improvement in the conduct and moral values of generations to come. This is in no way to imply that companies are alone in their sometimes wayward influence on students. There are many elements in society that contribute to moral decay. The parent who cheats on his income tax or boasts of putting in for overtime he did not work is equally guilty, but the excuse that "other people do it too" is a pathetically poor rationalization for any action which threatens to perpetuate dishonesty.

In his essay entitled "The Luxury of Integrity," Stuart Chase writes,

It is my contention that for uncounted millions of Americans the price of integrity is more than they can afford.

Living in a crowd, it has become highly important to fit in. There are fewer square holes for square pegs; to make the close-locked wheels of industry turn, an employee must be as round as a ball bearing. This smooth and oily quality that eases the friction of the highly organized machine is in a way more vital than professional training, ability, or energy. One man may be genial and tactful by nature, while nine have to achieve tact and geniality by effort. For the milk of human kindness the most obvious substitute is soft soap.[1]

Companies who enter into agreements with a university for the expressed purpose of contributing to the education of young people have a moral responsibility not to make the luxury of integrity too costly for these young people who are dependent on the successful completion of cooperative work experience.

THE STUDENT'S RESPONSIBILITY TO HIMSELF

Shakespeare's provocative adage, "to thine own self be true, And it must follow, as the night, the day, Thou canst not then be false to any man," should be the credo of every college student confronted with moral conflicts of any nature. Having chosen the Cooperative Plan of Education over the conventional four-year system, it behooves the student to make the most of what this "unconventional" system has to offer. Co-op is not just a convenient way of earning one's college expenses. Although a recent study indicated that 100 percent of the students questioned cited the "financial benefits of working

[1] Stuart Chase, *The Nemesis of American Business* (New York, 1931), pp. 29–30.

during college" as their reason for attending a co-op college, 98.3 percent also cited the "educational value of on-the-job experience."[2] The tangible nature of money may make it difficult at times for a student to see the intangible advantage of the educational experience, but this is part of the student's responsibility to mature from the childish inability to see anything but the immediately evident. The business student who regretted having to give up his summer job of "running a hot-dog stand down at the beach" because he earned $125 a week, had to learn that although running a hot-dog stand might entail some managerial problems, the experience would be of little value to the boy's future career in fire insurance!

Quite the reverse picture is presented by the student who becomes so practically oriented in his work experience that he loses his ability to think in the abstract. The student who attempts to translate every parcel of his textbook knowledge into some tangible, practical use is in danger of becoming narrow in his outlook and of missing some of the most exciting aspects of a university education. Students need to look for the fringe benefits on a job—the seemingly insignificant by-products that may in the long run prove more valuable than the primary experience itself. The history major who aspires to a teaching career but finds himself on co-op in a state school for the mentally retarded, can learn much about disciplining a class if he is willing to approach his job with a completely open mind.

The student whose career objectives are not well defined—and even the student who feels certain as to his ultimate goal—should learn to take advantage of the new career opportunities that may open up through what may seem to be unrelated cooperative assignments. A student who had no idea of devoting his life to the mentally retarded was so touched by the sight of a child's grief at his leaving that he gave up his original career objectives in order to devote his life to the education of handicapped youngsters.

The student who finds the academic side of college difficult also owes it to himself to persevere until he has had an opportunity to try his hand at working in a semiprofessional capacity. History is full of geniuses who failed more than one course in college, and the latent talents of an individual may show themselves in his work

[2] *Survey of Co-operative Education—Student's Viewpoint.* Student Committee for Co-operative Education, Northeastern University, Boston, Massachusetts.

rather than the classroom atmosphere. Youth is often impatient and unwilling to work for distant goals, but the student who will force himself to keep plugging may surprise himself in the long run, and then, and then only, will he realize how much he might have lost had he given up when the going was rough.

Patience often comes hard to the college student, and it may even plague the brilliant one who finds himself bored because his co-op job has given him knowledge beyond the level of classroom discussion. This is a nice kind of problem, however, as it stimulates individual study, and—more often than not—the boredom is momentary as the student finds that one of his classmates is now ahead of the class and it is he who must again study to keep up.

The question of personal ethics is also important in view of our previous discussion. Just as a company has responsibility not to tempt, the student has a responsibility not to be tempted. If previous generations have failed in this respect, as indeed there can be no question that they have, then perhaps it will be the privilege of the younger generation to lead the way back to the reestablishment of individual initiative and strength of character. We may not respect the image of Madison Avenue, and yet if we remain passive to its influence we are condoning its every method and device. Once again, here is knowledge to be gained from the words of Stuart Chase:

The yes man had no place in the pioneer tradition. The pioneer had his faults and virtues. The faults included a prodigal wastefulness, a disposition to befoul one nest and move on to the next, a certain laxity in respect to the social amenities. The virtues included a sturdy independence, and the compulsion, if need arose, to look every man level in the eye and tell him to go to hell. Reasonably secure in the fruits of his own labor and thus economically independent, he could express in any company his honest opinions as forcibly as he pleased, and, subject to the local *mores*—the base line from which all human behavior must stem —he could vote for candidates he respected, agitate for reforms he believed in, refuse to do jobs which galled his sense of decency or craftsmanship, come and go as the seasons dictated, but not at the bidding of any overlord. His opinions may have been frequently deplorable, his acts often crude and peremptory, but he was free to be true to the best he knew—and so, by the Eternal! a man and not a rubber stamp.[3]

Stuart Chase, *op. cit.*, p. 30.

[Editor's Note: This chapter is placed in an appendix since its con
tents has less general appeal. Yet the Cooperative Plan of Education
is neither new nor rare. Its inception dates back to 1906, and now
over a hundred institutions make the plan available in some form
The National Commission for Cooperative Education reports tha‍
the number of institutions adopting the principle is steadily increas
ing, both in the United States and in foreign countries. Dr. Ralph
W. Tyler, chairman of the Commission, has stated: "Cooperative
education gives a student an education qualitatively superior in
some respects to a conventional college education. Cooperative
students become more mature; and their records in graduate school
and in employment show that cooperative education is a first-rate
college education."[4]]

[4] Asa S. Knowles, *A College President Looks at Cooperative Education* (New York
1964), p. i.

II / Louis E. Reik, M.D.

TODAY'S STUDENT AND
THE COLLEGE PSYCHIATRIST*

At one time it was generally assumed that by the time an individual was 18, the main lines of his character were pretty well formed, a view that drew support from psychoanalytic theory, which stresses particularly the fateful importance of early childhood experiences. Therefore, the colleges, in spite of their professed interest in character formation, could more or less ignore the personality development of a student and concern themselves mainly with offering opportunities for his further intellectual growth along lines presumably already fixed. But recent extensive studies of normal college students clearly indicate that important emotional development and change occur during the college years.

These studies, begun in the 1930's with the pioneer work of Henry A. Murray at Harvard, have spread to other colleges, notably Vassar, and are currently in progress at Massachusetts Institute of Technology, Berkeley, Harvard, and elsewhere. Already they have disclosed much information, some of it of particular interest to parents and college psychiatrists. (It also has relevance for educators, since it raises questions of how the college can encourage desirable change.) We now realize, for instance, that *significant change even*

* Reprinted with permission from UNIVERSITY: A Princeton Quarterly, copyright © 1967, Princeton University.

in presumably normal students is apt to be accompanied by emotional upset. It seems that even the young are more conservative than they realize when faced with the need to put away childish things.

The case study of the Vassar student "Penny," appearing in Nevitt Sanford's recent book *Self and Society* (Atherton Press, N.Y., 1966), illustrates quite vividly—for Sanford somehow brings "Penny" alive in a way that most case studies fail to do—how and why students become upset and are obliged to change during their college years. Of primary importance is the realization that they want on the one hand to venture on the uncharted seas of maturity and on the other find themselves clinging to childish attitudes toward parents, parent-surrogates, and themselves. Though the upsets they experience can often be dealt with in other ways, they are painful enough to prompt students quite frequently to seek psychiatric help on their own initiative. And their seeking help is not necessarily a sign of weakness. On the contrary, it may reveal not only that the student has the courage and humility to face problems, but also that he is already well embarked on the journey to maturity; that he has more than average self-awareness and sensitivity to others. And these qualities partly explain why the student is often quick to respond to relatively little help.

That today's youth looks more favorably upon the psychiatrist than parents realize is shown in various ways. The number of college students seeking psychiatric help on their own initiative is steadily climbing. In the cities, psychiatric out-patient clinics and hospitals report so marked an increase in youthful patients that the more than 500 psychiatrists in this country concentrating on the study and treatment of adolescents are setting up special clinics and are forming a national society for adolescent psychiatry.

When the writer first came to Princeton in 1953, he began keeping careful statistics on the sourse of referral for the students who came to him, knowing, of course, that those who came on their own initiative were apt to be better motivated for help than the reluctant "captive" patients sent by parents or someone else in authority. The percentage of self-referred students has gradually risen from about 30% to the present level of over 50%, and the total number of students has more than doubled during a period when total undergraduate enrollment did not increase markedly. Other private institutions report the same trend, justifying the observation made a few years ago by Dr. Dana L. Farnsworth, director of Harvard health services, that any university adding another psychiatrist to its staff need not worry about keeping him busy.

Obviously, students are ceasing to think of the psychiatrist as a bogeyman whose domain is the mental hospital and who works primarily with the insane. And probably mainly because of the publicity given to psychoanalysis, which distinctly does not limit itself to severe psychopathology but attempts to contribute to normal psychology as well, college students today are apt to associate the psychiatrist with the psychoanalyst who sits quietly while his patients "free associate" about problems, the nature and origins of which he seeks to help them understand. He is pictured as a man to whom one goes for the purpose of dispelling the private mysteries of emotional entanglements—without one's giving up the idea of being, or becoming, fundamentally normal. This prevalent idea of normality as a relative state, contingent on the vicissitudes of emotional life, derives, of course, to a considerable extent from Freud.

Freud's pioneer observation that normal everyday life, not to mention the nightlife of dreams, can be strongly influenced, if only transiently, by the sometimes frightening and destructive power of irrational feeling has gradually opened the eyes of the informed public to the enormous amount of psychopathy stemming from emotionalism in persons who, because they are not psychotic by the traditional standards of hospital psychiatry, have been presumed to be normal. Moreover, students are becoming increasingly aware that the distortions and prejudices of emotionalism remain comparatively unaffected by exhortation and reasonable advice, but need to be seen in the perspective of an individual's changing personal desires and the past experiences that continue to influence him. Helping students to achieve this kind of understanding is the basic purpose of college psychiatry, which, though for practical reasons it cannot offer classical psychoanalytic treatment, borrow the psychoanalytic approach of searching for the how and why of emotional upset rather than merely observing and classifying symptoms and trying to suppress them with drugs or fatherly advice.

Intelligent students of today are more likely than their elders to understand Freud's proposition that to a degree we are all irrational; and they are increasingly confronted by evidence of this: wars, riots, smoke-ins, be-ins, and various Quixotic movements, violent and non-violent. Probably more than any generation before them, today's students, typically fascinated by the sensational and unusual, are becoming familiar with a broad range of psychopathology in man's nature—the intimate, uncanny experiences of schizophrenics, drug-addicts, pseudomystics, and sexual deviates. A profusion of books, films, plays, and surrealistic art is concerned with themes from man's underworld, in the manner of Hieronymus Bosch, Blake, the Marquis de Sade, Baudelaire, and Kafka: *Lolita, In Cold Blood, The Boston Strangler, Naked Lunch, Turned On, La Dolce Vita, Who's Afraid of Virginia Woolf?, I Never Promised You a Rose Garden*— all presenting vivid projections of "the flowers of evil" that can grow in man's subterranean life. And these works are at once enlightening and disturbing: enlightening insofar as they stimulate the wish to achieve understanding and rational control of powerful destructive forces in others and in one's self; disturbing because they dramatize the primitive power of desire to defy the restraints of reason and the logic of the mind.

Questions arise in students' minds as they become increasingly aware of what lies behind the masks people wear, questions reflecting their growing fascination with man's perennial problem of achieving the good life, or, in psychological terms, the normal life: *Is normality based on a statistical average? Is it a utopian dream, or is it something they can hope to achieve?*

Specifically, the questions take such forms as: *Is it normal to try LSD? To have sexual relations with a nice girl one does not love? To aspire to the unattainable as Don Quixote did? To live only for the moment, letting the past and future take care of themselves?*

It is not surprising, in view of today's concerns and the growing acceptance of modern psychiatry, that students seldom feel insulted by the suggestion that they seek psychiatric help. Nowadays, between 15% and 20% of the students at Harvard, Yale, and Princeton consult a college psychiatrist at some time during their four undergraduate years. Obviously, this does not mean that a sixth to a fifth of the students at these universities suffer significant psychiatric disability. The number found to be so psychologically incapacitated that withdrawal must be recommended has remained remarkably and consistently low for the past 15 years: approximately one out of every 250 of the total Princeton graduate and undergraduate population per year.

We would like to reduce even this small number—about 20 a year—who must leave for psychiatric reasons. When we study them, they turn out to be a mixed lot. For some, crisis strikes swiftly and overwhelmingly and could not possibly have been predicted on the basis of the biographical material which the health services and the university routinely have available. For others, troublesome symptoms have plainly been present for some time.

For example, in the case of some students who take psychedelic substances, drug-taking is merely another incident in longstanding attempts to cope with disturbing neurotic symptoms: unexplained anxiety, insomnia, depression, and, especially, feelings of alienation. The latter symptom can refer to a much more significant disturbance than the limited forms of alienation commonly encountered when students complain of boredom with their work, or disenchantment with conventional mores and traditions. In the case of some of the students who experiment with drugs, the sense of alienation has been found to be not only more intense but also more extensive, in that they feel a numbing detachment from the body and psychic life as well as from people and things in the outside world.

Recent interesting studies, such as those in the department of psychiatry at the Yale School of Medicine, suggest that these youths suffer from a psychopathology which often includes a profound sense of alienation, with a serious inability to form satisfying relations —or to be in rapport—with the adult world, and even with peers, in any sustained, mutually gratifying way. Faced with that difficulty, they resort to impersonal means, such as drugs, to achieve an artificial sense of being in mystic union with the environment—nature, their fellows, or their own subjective world. They tend to have, in addition, an ill-defined concept of the self, periods of deep depression and suicidal thoughts, ungratifying sexual adventures, and an "existential" philosophy that considers living only in the present worthwhile. They commonly blame the world for being out of step, a view that their elders sometimes hesitate to challenge. Thus they are reluctant to seek psychiatric help. When they do, they are difficult to treat.

Perhaps one generalization applies to the small group of students who develop significant psychiatric difficulty. Characteristically, they are resistant to psychiatric help—largely because self-"love" is so strong that they cannot endure self-criticism, even of those elements in themselves that are impairing their social life and their ability to learn. And it is, of course, this exaggerated defensiveness that makes them feel life would be unbearable if others knew about their private limitations.

Strangely enough, however, they sometimes respond, particularly when in deep trouble, to concerned insistence on the part of parents or friends that they visit a psychiatrist—if only to prove that he is powerless to help them! Occasionally they display surprising cooperation. Incidentally, psychiatrists are only too familiar with people who fundamentally consider themselves "non-patients," yet are not deterred on this account from returning repeatedly. Much of the work of the college psychiatrist has to do with helping refractory students clear away the obstacles that self-"love" sets up against awareness of self-defeating tendencies and inner misery. (The word "love" is quoted here because it is obviously not real love, which is a *healthful* attitude, even—or especially—toward one's self. "Love" —in quotes—is like infatuation which blindly cherishes, which admits no imperfections, which defends tendencies that work against the individual's own best interest. Gripped by self-"love," students overestimate their abilities and underestimate those of others, and persist in surrendering to impulse, regardless of consequences, on the grounds of the supremacy of personal desire over social taboos.)

Ideally, students ought to be as willing to consult college psychiatrists about psychological problems as they are to consult physicians about physical ailments—but they probably never will be. Self-"love" to some degree is, after all, universal, and no student tolerates easily the idea that his mind, the most precious possession of the educated man, functions defectively. Psychiatric experience teaches, however, that where self-"love" reaches such inflated proportions that students are unduly sensitive about psychiatric help though obviously in trouble, there are often concomitant strong feelings of self-hate, inferiority, or insecurity.

So much for the growing willingness of all but a small minority of students to take at least the initial steps towards psychiatric help. What about the attitude of their parents? On the whole, they give the impression of viewing it with alarm or at best having mixed feelings about it—certainly not surprising since psychiatric work deals with matters about which people *do* have strong feelings, whether of apprehension, pride, or prejudice. When parents are concerned about the possibility of a physical disorder in their children, they take straightforward action: They insist on a medical consultation if for no other reason than to relieve their own anxiety. They do not hesitate to discuss the facts of the case with a medical adviser.

But when the disorder is emotional, parents' mixed feelings are apt to express themselves in ways that help neither the student nor themselves—in a tendency toward concealment rather than frank recognition of emotional problems, and in inaction rather than alertness and action designed to be of help. For example, parents occasionally conceal entirely from the university health services the student's history of previous psychiatric treatment; or they propose unnecessarily complicated schemes to maneuver a student into the college psychiatrist's office with the stipulation that the student be kept in the dark about their concern and the reason for the visit. Extreme examples of this kind are the exception rather than the rule; but, if taken along with other indications of apprehension more frequently encountered, they testify to the reluctance of parents to suggest psychiatric help for a son or daughter in college.

It may be helpful to consider some of the reasons parents give for this reluctance:

ONE. *"Psychiatry as a science has a dubious status compared with other healing specialties: internists and surgeons, relying on technical data from laboratory and X-ray room, not to mention the lowly clinical thermometer, diagnose and treat their patients in tangible forms in contrast to the vague procedures of the psychiatrist."*

To this the psychiatrist replies that medical men are becoming increasingly aware of the dangers of ignoring the patient while concentrating on the technical ramifications of his disease, in the manner demanded by the twentieth-century idols of exact science and technology. Precisely because his data are drawn from two worlds—one of observable phenomena and the other of feeling and ideas—the psychiatrist's opportunity of achieving harmony between the two is enhanced. In the unseen world of the mind, the capricious and conflicting feelings that motivate men defy measurement. But dramatists, poets, religious men, and humanists have taught us too much about the importance of feelings for science to downgrade them because they are subjective and can only be inferred.

Not only does the inner world exist, but out of its interaction with the tangible outside world comes creativity as well as neurosis. Either the individual alters the outside world, or by submitting to it becomes altered himself. And just as the outside world resists the individual's attempts to change it, so does the individual's inner world oppose change from without. While creativity can result from a happy resolution of this tension, more often the result is unhappy compromise or neurosis, the latter occurring when the attempt to harmonize contradictory private tendencies is governed by the wishful naïveté of childhood rather than by the realities of adult life.

It is a curious paradox that a student's inner life of feeling and sensation can be more real and meaningful to him than the most exact scientific data about material objects that evoke little or no concern in his mind. The importance of the inner world as the source of life's meaning has led philosophers like Bertrand Russell and William James to postulate two forms of knowledge: one consisting of descriptive knowledge *about* things, to which the exact scientist devotes himself; the other of a more intimate knowing through actual inner experience. Indeed, Sir Julian Huxley called on education to recognize a "curriculum of experience as well as a curriculum of subjects." And Mark Twain observed, "A fellow who takes hold of a bull by the tail, once, is getting sixty or seventy times as much information as the fellow who hasn't."

A conspicuous minority of today's students has been attempting to enhance inner experience by methods almost as extreme as the one cited by Mark Twain. Sometimes they become so immersed in the inner life that they carelessly overlook the dangers of going against ordinary commonsense. They experiment with dangerous drugs like LSD, become fascinated with mysticism, with the mysteries of hypnosis and psychoanalysis; or, adopting an extreme position which they believe derives from existentialism, they hold that external life is an absurd nothing, and inner being is everything; that, indeed, Camus was right in insisting that Sisyphus, whose mission of endlessly rolling a rock up a hill was constantly frustrated, was nevertheless happy.

Some parents regard this as evidence of morbid introspection, and fear it will only be encouraged by psychiatry. They maintain that the chief task of a student is to achieve successful adaptation to the hard realities of a competitive world; that the private world of introspection must give way to everyday practicalities and effective action.

As is often the case when feelings run high between the generations, each side refuses to concede that the other is partly right.

The college psychiatrist joins those who since Socrates have recognized that not all introspection is morbid; there is also a healthy kind that tries to eliminate self-deception arising from emotional bias, so that action will be more fitting and just.

TWO. *"Sure, psychiatric help is fine for abnormal people, but unnecessary if not harmful for a normal college student."*

Unfortunately, the psychiatrist can no more give a precise general definition of "normality" than of the old term "insanity." He must insist instead on the separate consideration of individual cases, and he holds that normality sometimes *includes* the presence of sufficient emotional upset and suffering to make psychiatric help desirable. He does not, however, disagree with the common sense of parents which tells them that a reasonable amount of anxiety, instead of calling for psychiatric help, may stimulate the student to deal effectively with his ordeals.

But if the right amount of anxiety can stimulate, too much of it can paralyze. Take the case of a graduate student who sought psychiatric help on his own initiative because his attempts to prepare for the concluding phase of his work has evoked such an unbearable sense of inadequacy and dread of the examination ordeal—accompanied by fatigue, insomnia, and marked loss of appetite—that he could do no work at all. Reactions of this kind do not always indicate a chronic incapacity. This man, when last heard from, was doing well in business. What he mainly came to realize in a series of psychiatric visits was that he had been trapped by a combination of external pressures from parents, teachers, and friends into seeking something which, belatedly, he discovered he hated. He was, in Wordsworth's phrase, "more like a man / Flying from something that he dreads . . . than one / Who sought the thing he loved." The fact that he had allowed himself to fall into this trap argued a flaw in his nature, but not an incurable one. Cases like this reassure the psychiatrist that "normality" can be determined only by viewing present symptoms and inner weakness in a context of external influences and inner strength.

THREE. *"Psychiatry is a form of 'coddling,' encouraging dependency in students and thus sapping their will to learn for themselves in the school of hard knocks."*

True, the experience of failure does go deep, especially when never experienced before, and thus can be a better teacher than success. True, too, what a student learns for himself is often more precious than what some authority tells him; indeed, authority can be an obstacle to those wanting to learn. *But what the psychiatrist focuses on is not failure as such but why it occurred and, above all, whether the student has the ability and insight to convert that failure into an experience of learning and growth.*

In general, the college psychiatrist is less concerned than parents and professors with a student's having an isolated and apparently inexplicable failure in his academic work, or even with his dropping out of college. Studies of dropouts (*The College Dropout and the Utilization of Talent*, Princeton University Press, 1966) indicate that these failures sometimes have a beneficial effect. To the degree that they generate self-knowledge, there is, as Salvador Dali maintains, something "sacred" about mistakes.

But perhaps no one knows better than college psychiatrists and deans, from their experience with many students who in one way or another have failed, that the ability to learn from mistakes is precisely what separates those students who don't need help from those who do. For one conspicuous mark of neurotic behavior is its repetitive, automatic quality that eludes control despite resolutions and apparently sincere attempts to correct it. The fact that it originates in submerged tendencies outside of awareness only makes it more incomprehensible to parents and an additional source of anxiety to students.

Because his neurotic tendencies are submerged, a student has trouble seeing that they are simultaneously sources of gratification (to the childish elements in his personality) and anxiety (to the part of his psyche that wants to grow up); that an archaic or childish part of him is at war with a maturing process. As a result, the worry arising from these submerged sources not only tends to revolve in vicious circles but also is frequently misdiagnosed, as when a dental patient incriminates a sound tooth and is surprised when the dentist discovers that another, quite removed, is the source of pain. Thus if asked to explain their failure, these students commonly attribute it to superficial causes or admit they *can't* explain it. Parents are apt to suggest that the student simply try to forget his worry, or escape it through work or recreation.

The psychiatrist has no quarrel with this advice—if it works. But when it doesn't, and the student continues to show signs of being overwhelmed by worry to the point where it spoils what he previously enjoyed or even impairs his health, then simply admonishing him may only make matters worse. *It is at this point that the student in his misery not only needs but ordinarily will accept help from the college psychiatrist.*

FOUR. *"The psychiatric approach, particularly in cases of misbehavior or delinquency, undermines or tries to circumvent campus regulations or the laws of the land by pleading for exemption on the grounds of illness. The appropriate disciplinary action will provide the cure for the erring student."*

Needless to say, this view is more frequently heard from those charged with upholding college standards and the law than from parents. But some parents do voice it.

Actually, the college psychiatrist, dealing as he does largely with students at the normal end of the continuum, rarely encounters one who, charged with some offense, expects immunity from disciplinary action on the grounds of illness; nor is the psychiatrist likely to involve himself in the question of whether disciplinary action should be taken, a decision that belongs to the community, with which he is ready, however, to work in a consulting capacity. What concerns the psychiatrist is the nature of the student's problems and his long range psychological needs. Just as the administration must sometimes make the difficult choice of placing the welfare of the institution above that of the individual, so the psychiatrist's duty is first and foremost to the individual.

The chief disadvantage of the "cure" by punishment is that it is apt to be only temporary, particularly in students with deeply ingrained neurotic tendencies. To such students their own misbehavior —compulsive neglect of curriculum, exhibitionism, stealing, or sexual promiscuity—has an alien quality, so that they can neither explain it nor excuse it. Far from attempting to defend themselves, they seem almost eager for punishment. After society has exacted its penalty, they are left with the illusion that all is well, and lose the incentive to seek psychiatric help if not encouraged to do so.

Ideally, of course, the college psychiatrist's function should complement, not replace, that of parents and administrative authorities, with whom he and the student work out whatever program seems in the student's best interest. Parents and the administration, for their part, should view the offending student not simply in terms of his offense but also with the possibility in mind that he is reacting to neurotic, self-defeating tendencies which punishment alone will not remedy.

There are, of course, student offenders who despite obviously self-defeating actions insist on their normality and resist psychiatric help. For both parents and psychiatrist they pose a difficult problem. The danger is that these students, who seem to speak sincerely and plausibly of their ability to control their behavior in the future, will persuade both parents and psychiatrist to be falsely optimistic, even when there have been repeated offenses in the past.

Though psychiatrists are naturally reluctant to accept resistant patients, they nevertheless have a duty to assess as thoroughly as possible the life history of such students, both for clues to their psychopathology and for ways of effecting a meeting of minds. Sometimes these young people, wearing what has been called the "mask of sanity," are found to have not only an apparent absence of remorse but an inability to reflect and to explain themselves in language meaningful to others, though they may be fluent enough on a superficial level. The mystery of why some parents are willing to be so tolerant of young people of this kind intrigues the psychiatrist. A possible answer may lie in the recent provocative clinical report which concluded that the patients studied were acting out the unconscious fantasies and unacceptable impulses of their own parents!

FIVE. *"A psychiatric consultation, to say nothing of treatment, will be a permanent blemish on a student's record."*

Parents—and sometimes students themselves—who voice this fear simply do not understand that the college psychiatrist's first duty is to his patient; that only when his patient actively threatens serious harm to himself or to others will the psychiatrist depart from the rules that for centuries have governed the confidentiality of the physician-patient relationship—and then, preferably, only with the patient's knowledge, if not consent. Fortunately, college faculty and administrators, being keenly aware of the confidential relationship that a psychiatrist must maintain with student-patients, neither insist on knowing which students consult him nor expect information about which the latter might be sensitive. But even so, the best safeguard of the student's privacy is the policy at Princeton and elsewhere of releasing information only with the knowledge *and* consent of the student, except, as mentioned above, in cases of imminent danger.

SIX. *"We are a church-going family, and would rather have our son talk over his problems with his chaplain than with a psychiatrist."*

The psychiatrist has several reasons for respecting the parents' preference, particularly when it coincides with the student's. The latter may find it easier to talk candidly with a chaplain about personal matters than to a psychiatrist or anyone else. Often what the student needs more than technical interpretations from the psychiatrist is a thorough airing, with a friendly and responsible adult, of problems he otherwise would have to endure in loneliness. And it is, of course, a good guiding principle to encourage students to consult those they like and trust. The experienced chaplain can be counted on to suggest psychiatric consultation if it seems needed.

SEVEN. *"Our son has always talked very freely with us, and if he is in any difficulty we would rather have him discuss it with us than with a psychiatrist."*

It is good from a mental health point of view for students to be able to talk freely with parents about their difficulties, for it provides a safety-valve for the release of pent-up worries. But parents are apt to be at a disadvantage in discussing certain types of problems with their sons or daughters. One reason is that in late adolescence difficulties commonly center around the intimate sexual sphere and are embarrassing for students and parents to discuss together, with the result that they are seldom aired at all. Not infrequently, a student will tell the psychiatrist that the very closeness of his relationship with his parents makes him prefer not to discuss such problems with them for fear of upsetting them.

A second reason is that the normal trend of youthful development is away from unquestioning acceptance of parental values, and toward the forging of an independent value-system and identity. Though college students like to imagine, with bravado, that they are mature, one of their most complicated and distressing tasks is to overcome the feelings of dependency and helplessness they had in the long years of childhood—feelings that continue to haunt them even on the threshold of adulthood.

A third reason is that the student is sometimes best helped by talking with someone who is emotionally neutral, an attitude which the psychiatrist, like the scientist, cultivates in his search for objective truth. This attitude is seldom possible, desirable, or helpful in parents, who, when they attempt to conceal strong feelings from their offspring, may only bewilder or antagonize them.

Now a word about that small minority of parents who are too eager to assume that their sons and daughters need such help; who, out of an exaggerated sense of guilt for parental shortcomings, real or imagined, are both over-concerned about the welfare of their children and perhaps too anxious to make their troubles known. Some divorced parents, aware of statistics about how children are damaged by a broken home, not only alert various members of the college staff but also volunteer detailed information about the broken home from which the student comes.

The psychiatrist must tell such parents that much as he would like to be able to find, through statistical studies, some infallible determinants of emotional illness, the fact remains that individuals vary widely in their ability to cope with trouble. Some, far from being overwhelmed, seem to derive from it the impetus for creative activity.

Recently, Ian Gregory, chairman of the Department of Psychiatry at Ohio State University College of Medicine, studied a group of undergraduates at Carleton, a small coeducational college, to determine how the loss of a parent by death or divorce affected them. He found "a much higher frequency of parental loss by divorce and a somewhat higher frequency of parental loss by death during childhood" among students who consulted the college psychiatrist than among the general student population—*but* they included "a number of students with relatively trivial emotional problems." Perhaps a more important finding was the absence of any relationship between the loss of a parent and graduation status. Indeed, two of the four males graduating summa cum laude had lost a parent by death during childhood, suggesting that factors associated with bereavement "may lead some students to strive for exceptional achievement."

These rather unexpected findings do not, of course, mean that a broken home is not a drawback to many children. But they remind all of us of the dangers of generalizing. (A handicap is sometimes offset by an advantage, and the child of divorced parents may enjoy superior economic and cultural status.)

Though graduation from college is not the equivalent of achieving eminence in later life, the provocative point that adversity may provide the stimulus for achievement is made over and over in the numerous studies that have been appearing lately of outstanding men. The Goertzels in their study of 400 famous men and women, *Cradles of Eminence* (Little, Brown and Company, 1962), make the following comments:

Three-fourths of the children are troubled—by poverty; by a broken home; by rejecting, over-possessive, estranged, or dominating parents; by financial ups and downs; by physical handicaps or by parental dissatisfaction over the children's school failures or vocational choices. . . . It may be currently possible to be both creative and comfortable. We suspect it isn't, but our suspicions are not scientific data.

Of course, this kind of study neither solves the riddle of greatness nor advocates hardship in childhood as a necessary pre-condition for it.

So much for parents who are too ready to arrange psychiatric help for a student, and for those who are too reluctant: What of the parents who are prejudiced in neither direction, but are simply puzzled as to whether a student needs, or would be materially helped by, psychiatric consultation? What clues or symptoms might these parents be guided by?

First, a student will benefit from psychiatric consultation *if he believes that he will*. Whether he arrives at this belief easily, because of a longstanding but unrecognized habit of dependency, or reluctanctly, because it conflicts with the urge to independence, his own decision to consult the psychiatrist, more than anything the psychiatrist says or does, may mark the turning-point towards willingness to face problems. It should be respected.

Second, if a student's problems are causing trouble in more than one of the four major areas—working, playing, eating, sleeping— he probably needs help. The student whose work is going poorly but is not killing his enjoyment of extra-curricular activities, and is not interfering with his appetite and sleep, probably can straighten things out by himself or with the help of parents, adviser, chaplain or friends. But if his work is going poorly *and* he has lost his zest for life, or is eating and sleeping badly, his problem may be more deep-seated.

Parents would be well advised to respect expressions of concern by a student's friends or adviser—just as the psychiatrist is well advised to heed expressions of concern from parents—because those who know the student well have the tremendous advantage, from a preventive standpoint, of being able to detect trouble in its early stages; to judge from knowledge of the students' background how seriously the trouble is likely to affect him.

As the role of the college psychiatrist becomes better understood by all concerned, the question of "to consult or not to consult" will become easier to answer—and less momentous. The first visit to the psychiatrist will be undertaken more informally; and if, as will often be the case, student and psychiatrist decide together that further visits are *not* called for, nothing will have been lost. If both decide that psychiatric help *is* indicated, much will have been gained.

THE AUTHORS

JOSEPH C. BENTLEY (B.A., M.A., PH.D.) is Professor of Educational Psychology at the University of Utah. He has been a National Science Fellow, Danforth Graduate Fellow, and National Institute of Mental Health Post-Doctoral Fellow. He has also served on the faculty at Clark University, the University of Minnesota, and as Visiting Professor at Holy Cross College. As Consultant and Professor, first with KTCA-TV Educational Television at St. Paul, and then with the Ministry of Education in Venezuela, Dr. Bentley has given added dimensions to his career.

WILLIAM J. BOWERS (B.A., PH.D.) is Director of Research of the Russell B. Stearns Study and Professor of Sociology at Northeastern University. He is the author of the definitive work on college cheating, *Student Dishonesty and Its Control in College.* Published by the Bureau of Applied Social Research at Columbia University and supported by the United States Office of Education, this study has received widespread attention. He is currently directing a nationwide research and action program on other aspects of campus behavior, including the current phenomenon of student power.

CHARLES W. HAVICE (A.B., M.A., S.T.B., PH.D., D.D.) is the Dean of Chapel, and Professor of Philosophy and Religion at Northeastern University where he received a citation for distinguished teaching. He is a former president of the National Association of College and University Chaplains, an executive committee member of the Association for the Coordination of University Religious Affairs, and is active in other campus-related organizations. As Chairman of the Russell B. Stearns Study he has visited over sixty colleges and universities.

RICHARD F. HETTLINGER (M.A.) was born in England and was graduated with honors from Cambridge University. He is an Episcopal priest and has taught in Toronto, Canada; at the Central College of the Anglican Communion in Canterbury, England; and at the Graduate School of Ecumenical Studies in Geneva, Switzerland. After graduate work at Yale he became Chaplain of Kenyon College, Gambier, Ohio, where his interest in problems of sexuality led to the publications of *Living with Sex: The Student's Dilemma* (New York, 1967). He is now Professor of Religion at Kenyon and a Consulting Editor for the journal *Medical Aspects of Human Sexuality*.

RONALD E. A. JACKSON (B.S., M.S., ED.D.) is the Associate Dean of Students at the University of Rochester. He formerly served as Assistant Dean of Students at Kansas State University, Dean of Men at American University, and Dean of Students at the University of North Dakota. Dean Jackson is past Associate Editor for the *Journal of College Student Personnel*, a member of the advisory board of *Off to College*, and a representative from the American College Personnel Association to the Senate of the American Guidance and Personnel Association.

GILBERT G. MAC DONALD (B.I.E., ED.M.) is Vice President for Student Affairs and the Dean of Students at Northeastern University, where he also holds the faculty appointment of Professor of Education. For over a score of years he has been closely related to student life on the campus, earlier serving respectively as Assistant Director of Admissions, Assistant Dean of Students, and Dean of Freshmen. He was also an Educational Consultant in the United States Navy serving as Communications Officer with the rank of Lieutenant, Senior Grade. A long-time member of the National Association of Student Personnel Administrators, he has been active on several of its national committees.

RAYMOND O. MURPHY (B.S., M.ED., D.ED.) is Dean of Men at The Pennsylvania State University in University Park, Pennsylvania. He also serves part-time on the faculty of that institution as an Assistant Professor of Education. Dr. Murphy is currently President of The Pennsylvania Association of Student Personnel Administrators and is the Institutional Delegate to the National Association of Student Personnel Administrators. He has authored several papers on the administration of student programs with particular emphasis on residence halls. He annually directs a conference on student life in residence halls for administrators from other colleges. In his present position Dr. Murphy has had the opportunity to know and work closely with hundreds of Penn State men and women as they pursue their degrees.

LOUIS E. REIK (A.B., M.D.) is Chief Psychiatrist in Princeton's Health Services, where his help is available to undergraduates, graduate students, and

Princeton Theological Seminary students. He is associated with Princeton Community Hospital. Author of various papers on mental health problems and the history of psychiatry, he co-edited (with Lawrence A. Pervin and Dr. Willard Dalrymple) *The College Dropout and the Utilization of Talent* (Princeton University Press, 1966).

NEVITT SANFORD (B.A., M.A., PH.D.) is Professor of Psychology and Education and Director of the Institute for the Study of Human Problems at Stanford University. He has been a prison psychologist, a practicing psychoanalyst, and a director of major studies in child development, personality assessment, political and social attitudes, the social psychology of higher education, alcoholism and other alcohol related problems. His numerous publications in the field of personality and social psychology include his contributions to H. A. Murray's *Explorations in Personality* (1938), S. Koch's *Psychology: A Study of a Science* (1961), and B. Wolman's *Handbook of Clinical Psychology* (1965). He was editor and senior author of *Physique, Personality and Scholarship* (1943), *The Authoritarian Personality* (1950), *The American College* (1962), and *College and Character* (1964). He has prepared the article on "The field of personality" for the Encyclopedia of the Social Sciences. His latest books are *Self and Society* (1966) and *Where Colleges Fail* (1967).

RAY F. SHURTLEFF (B.A., ED.M.) formerly served as a Research Fellow on the Russell B. Stearns Study and a Residence Counselor at Northeastern University. His academic and R.O.T.C. career as an undergraduate was marked with distinction. He has served as a member of the Administrative Staff on the President's Commission on the Assassination of President Kennedy and as an Archives Student Trainee in the Office of Presidential Libraries at the National Archives and Records Service in Washington, D.C.

HERBERT H. STROUP (A.B., B.D., D.S.S.) is Dean of Students at Brooklyn College of the City University of New York. He is also Chairman of the Department of Personnel Service and Professor of Sociology and Anthropology. Among his many affiliations are the following: Fellow of the National Council on Religion and Higher Education, member of the Board of Trustees of the American Association for Middle East Studies, and a member of the Executive Committee of Church World Service. His most recent book is *Bureaucracy in Higher Education*. Earlier volumes include *Symphony of Prayer, Social Work: An Introduction to the Field*, and *Community Welfare Organization*. He serves on several editorial boards and frequently contributes journal articles of both professional and popular nature.

PHILIP A. TRIPP (A.M., PH.D.) is Vice President for Student Development at Georgetown University. He was formerly Specialist for Student Services in the Bureau of Higher Education in the United States Office of Education, Washington, D.C., and then Research Coordinator for the Bureau of Research in their Office of Education. Beginning his professional career as Professor of English at Shimer College, Dr. Tripp later served as a Research Associate at the University of Chicago, Counselor at the Chicago Teachers College, and Dean of Students at Washburn University.

WALTER D. WAGONER (B.A., B.D., TH.M., D.D.) is the Director of the Boston Theological Institute. Before accepting his present post, he served briefly as the Dean of the Graduate Theological Union and earlier for an extended time as the Executive Director of The Rockefeller Brothers Fund for Theological Education. Dr. Wagoner has also held chaplaincies in the United States Navy, and at Yale University, Colby College, and Northwestern University. His two latest books are *The Seminary* and *Bitter-Sweet Grace.*

JOY D. WINKIE (B.A., M.A.) is Editorial Assistant to the President at Northeastern University. She was formerly the Associate Director of Publications. Upon completing graduate work in journalism, she entered the field professionally. Miss Winkie is a member of the honorary journalistic society of Kappa Tau Alpha, the professional journalistic sorority of Theta Sigma Phi (former president of the Boston Chapter), and the Institute of Journalists, London, England. Her ability is well demonstrated in *Stepping Stones or Stumbling Blocks* published in 1965.

BIBLIOGRAPHY

ALLPORT, GORDON W., *The Individual and His Religion* (New York, 1956).
AMERICAN COUNCIL ON EDUCATION, *The Student in Higher Education* (Washington, 1965).
ASHBY, NEAL, "How Much Freedom Should College Students Have?" *Boston Sunday Globe*, March 7, 1965.
ASHER, HARRY, "They Split My Personality," *Saturday Review*, 46 (June 1, 1963), pp. 39–43.
Atlantic Monthly, "Troubled Campus," by the Editors of the *Atlantic Monthly* (Boston, 1966).
AVERILL, LLOYD J., *A Strategy for the Protestant College* (Philadelphia, 1966).
BAILEY, DERRICK SHERWIN, *The Mystery of Love and Marriage* (New York, 1952).
BARTON, ALLEN H. and PAUL S. LAZARSFIELD, *Studying the Effects of College Education: A Methodological Examination of Changing Values in College* (New Haven, Connecticut: The Hazen Foundation, 1954).
BEACH, WALDO, *Conscience on Campus* (New York, 1958).
BECKER, CARL L., *Freedom and Responsibility in the American Way of Life* (New York, 1958).
BELLMAN, SAMUEL I., (ed.). *The College Experience* (San Francisco, 1962).
BENDER, RICHARD N., (ed.). *On the Work of the Ministry in University Communities* (Nashville, 1962).
BERGER, PETER L., *The Noise of Solemn Assemblies* (New York, 1961).
BERTOCCI, PETER A., *Sex, Love, and the Person* (New York, 1967).
BERTON, PIERRE, *The Comfortable Pew* (Philadelphia, 1965).
BLAINE, GRAHAM, *Youth and the Hazards of Affluence* (New York, 1967).
BLOY, MYRON B., JR., *The Crisis of Cultural Change* (New York, 1965).
BONJEAN, CHARLES M. and REECE MC GEE, "Scholastic Dishonesty Among

177

Undergraduates in Differing Systems of Social Control," *Sociology of Education*, Winter, 1965, pp. 127–137.

BOWERS, WILLIAM J., "Cheating on the College Campus," NEA Journal, February, 1966, pp. 20–22.

────── *Student Dishonesty and Its Control in College* (New York, 1964).

BREEDLOVE, WILLIAM and JERRY E., *The Swinging Set* (Los Angeles, 1965).

BRILL, EARL H., *Sex Is Dead and Other Post Mortems* (New York, 1967).

BROOKOVER, WILBUR B., *et al.*, *The College Student* (New York, 1965).

CALDERONE, MARY S., *Release From Sexual Tensions* (New York, 1960).

CANTELON, JOHN E., *Protestant Approach to the Campus Ministry* (Philadelphia, 1964).

CAPON, ROBERT F., *Bed and Board: Plain Talk About Marriage* (New York, 1905).

CHAMBERLIN, JOHN GORDON, *Churches and the Campus* (Philadelphia, 1963).

CHESSER, EUSTACE, *Unmarried Love* (New York, 1965).

CHILD STUDY ASSOCIATION CONFERENCE: 1966, *Sex Education and the New Morality: Proceedings* (New York, 1967).

COHEN, MITCHELL, and DENNIS HALE, *The New Student Left* (Boston, 1966).

COLEMAN, JOHN, *The Task of the Christian in the University* (New York, 1947).

COX, HARVEY, *The Secular City* (New York, 1965).

CUNINGGIM, MERRIMON, *The College Seeks Religion* (New Haven, 1947).

DABNEY, VIRGINIUS, "Cheating Can Be Stopped," *Saturday Review*, May 21, 1966, pp. 68–69, 77.

DANIELS, EDGAR F., "The Dishonest Term Paper," *College English*, April, 1960, pp. 403–405.

DE ROPP, R., *Drugs and the Mind* (New York, 1957).

DOESCHER, W. O., *The Church College in Today's Culture* (Minneapolis, 1963).

DRAPER, HAL, *Berkeley: The New Student Revolt* (New York, 1965).

DUVALL, EVELYN R., *Why Wait Till Marriage?* (New York, 1965).

EARLE, NICK, *What's Wrong With the Church?* (Baltimore, 1961).

EARNSHAW, GEORGE L., *et al.*, *The Campus Ministry* (Valley Forge, 1964).

EDDY, EDWARD D., JR., "Do the Colleges Expect Enough? The Contribution the Colleges Can Make to Excellence in Character and Intellect." *Journal of Higher Education*, XXX, March, 1959, pp. 155–160.

────── *The College Influence on Student Character* (Washington, D.C.: American Council on Education, 1959).

ELLIS, ALBERT, *Sex and the Single Man* (New York, 1963).

ELLISON, JEROME, "American Disgrace: College Cheating," *Saturday Evening Post*, January 9, 1960, pp. 58–59.

FLETCHER, JOSEPH, *Situation Ethics* (Philadelphia, 1966).

—— *Moral Responsibility: Situation Ethics at Work* (Philadelphia, 1967).

FREEDMAN, MERVIN, and HARVEY POWELSON, "Drugs on Campus: Turned On and Turned Out." *Nation*, 202, January 31, 1966, pp. 25–26.

FRIEDENBERG, EDGAR Z., *Coming of Age in America* (New York, 1965).

FRIEDLANDER, ALBERT H., (ed.). *Never Trust a God Over 30* (Boston, 1967).

FROMM, ERICH, *The Art of Loving* (New York and Evanston, 1962).

GIBBS, MARK and T. RALPH MORTON, *God's Frozen People* (Philadelphia, 1964).

GIBSON, D. L., "Our Colleges and Moral Leadership," *Association of American Colleges Bulletin*, May 1952, pp. 347–353.

GOLDSEN, ROSE K., *et al*, *What College Students Think* (Princeton, N.J., 1960).

GREENE, GAEL, *Sex and the College Girl* (New York, 1964).

GROUP FOR THE ADVANCEMENT OF PSYCHIATRY, *Sex and the College Student* (New York: Group for the Advancement of Psychiatry, 1965).

HAMILL, ROBERT H., *Gods of the Campus* (New York, 1949).

HARP, JOHN and PHILIP TAIETY, "Academic Integrity and Social Structure: A Study of Cheating Among College Students," *Social Problems*, Spring, 1966, pp. 365–373.

HARTSHORNE, HUGH and MARK A. MAY, *Studies in Deceit*, Books I and II (New York, 1928).

HARTZELL, KARL D. and HARRISON SASSCER (editors), *The Study of Religion on the Campus Today* (Washington, D.C., 1967).

THE EDWARD W. HAZEN FOUNDATION, *College Reading and Religion* (New Haven, 1948).

HEATH, DOUGLAS H., *Explorations of Maturity* (New York, 1965).

HECHINGER, GRACE, "College Morals Mirror Our Society." *New York Times*, CXII, April 14, 1963.

HEDLEY, GEORGE, *Religion on Campus* (New York, 1955).

HERBERG, WILL, *Protestant-Catholic-Jew* (New York, 1955).

HETTLINGER, RICHARD F., *Living With Sex: The Student's Dilemma* (New York, 1966).

HOFFMAN, HANS, *Sex Incorporated: A Positive View of the Sexual Revolution* (Boston, 1967).

HULME, WILLIAM E., *Youth Considers Sex* (Camden, N.J., 1965).

HUNT, EVERETT LEE, *The Revolt of the College Intellectual* (Chicago, 1964).

JACOB, PHILIP E., *Changing Values in College* (New York, 1957).

KATOPE, CHRISTOPHER G. and PAUL G. ZOLBRAD, *Beyond Berkeley* (Cleveland, 1966).

KEATS, JOHN, *The Sheepskin Psychosis* (New York, 1963).

KEMP, CHARLES F., *Counseling with College Students* (Englewood Cliffs, N.J., 1966).

KENNISTON, KENNETH, *The Uncommited: Alienated Youth in American Society* (New York, 1965).

KERR, CLARK, *Uses of the University* (Cambridge, Mass., 1963).

KIRKENDALL, LESTER, *Premarital Intercourse and Interpersonal Relationships* (New York, 1966).

KNOWLES, ASA S., *A College President Looks at Co-operative Education* (New York, 1964).

LAWLER, JUSTICE G., *The Catholic Dimension in Higher Education* (Westminster, Maryland, 1959).

LERNER, JEREMY, "College Drug Scene." *Atlantic*, 216, November, 1965, pp. 127–130.

LEUBA, CLARENCE, *Effective Learning and Co-operative Education* (New York: National Commission for Co-operative Education, 1964).

LIGON, ERNEST W., *Dimensions of Character* (New York, 1956).

LINDEY, ALEXANDER, *Plagiarism and Originality* (New York, 1952).

LINEBERRY, WILLIAM P. (ed.), *Colleges at the Crossroads* (New York, 1966).

LIPTON, LAWRENCE, *Erotic Revolution* (Los Angeles, 1965).

LLOYD-JONES, ESTHER M. and HERMAN A. ESTRIN, *The American Student and His College* (Boston, 1967).

LUDER, WILLIAM FAY, *A New Approach to Sex* (Boston, 1966).

MALLERY, DAVID, *Ferment on the Campus* (New York, 1965).

MARTIN, JOHN M., *Juvenile Vandalism* (Springfield, Illinois, 1961).

MASTERS, WILLIAM H. and V. A. JOHNSON, *Human Sexual Response* (Boston, 1966).

MC CLUSKEY, NEIL G., S.J. (ed.), *Catholic Education in America* (New York, 1964).

MC COY, CHARLES S. and NEELY D. MC CARTER, *The Gospel on Campus* (Richmond, 1959).

MC LEAN, MILTON D. (ed.), *Religious Studies in Public Universities* (Carbondale, Ill., 1967).

MEAGHER, MARGARET C., "The Plagiarists!" *Catholic World*, February, 1938, pp. 585–591.

MEETH, L. RICHARD, *The Religious Factor in Faculty Selection and Retention in Protestant Colleges* (New York, 1965).

MERRIAM, THORNTON WARD, *Religious Counseling of Students* (Washington, 1943).

METHVIN, EUGENE H., "Behind Those Campus Demonstrations," *Reader's Digest*, Vol. 88, January, 1966, pp. 43–48.

MICHAELSEN, ROBERT, *The Study of Religion in American Universities* (New Haven, 1965).

MILLER, M. V. and S. GILMORE (eds.), *Revolution at Berkeley* (New York, 1965).

MILLET, JOHN D. *et al, What's A College For?* (Washington, D.C.: Public Affairs Press, 1961).

NATIONAL INTERFRATERNITY CONFERENCE, *Enduring Values in the College Fraternity* (New York, n.d.).

———— *Should My Student Join a Fraternity at College?* (New York, 1966).

———— *Should Your Son Join a Fraternity?* (New York, 1965).

NEWCOMB, THEODORE, *College Peer Groups: Problems and Prospects for Research* (Chicago, 1966).

NORTHEASTERN UNIVERSITY, *The Campus Ministry* (Boston, 1965).

———— *Northeastern University Co-operative Education Handbook* (Boston, 1965).

PELIKAN, JAROSLAV, *et al, Religion and the University* (Toronto, 1964).

PERRY, JOHN D., JR., *The Coffee House Ministry* (Richmond, Va., 1966).

PHILLIPS, JOHN B., *Your God Is Too Small* (New York, 1953).

PIKE, JAMES ALBERT, *Teen Agers and Sex* (Englewood Cliffs, N.J., 1965).

———— *You and the New Morality* (New York, 1967).

RAIMI, RALPH A., "Cheating in College," *Harper's Magazine*, May, 1966, pp. 68–70ff.

RIESMAN, DAVID, *Constraint and Variety in American Education* (New York, 1958).

———— "Student Culture and Faculty Values," *Spotlight on the College Student* (Washington, D.C.: American Council on Education, 1959).

RIVLIN, HARRY N. (ed.), *The First Years in College* (Boston, 1965).

ROBINSON, JOHN A. T., *Honest To God* (Philadelphia, 1963).

———— *But That I Can't Believe!* (New York, 1967).

ROBINSON, LEONARD, "Hearing Color, Smelling Music, Touching a Scent." *New York Times Magazine*, August 22, 1965, p. 14.

ROBSON, JOHN, *Educating for Brotherhood* (Menasha, Wis., 1965).

———— (ed.), *The College Fraternity and Its Modern Role* (Menasha, Wis., 1966).

———— (ed.), *Baird's Manual of American College Fraternities*, Seventeenth Edition (Menasha, Wis., 1963).

RUSSELL B. STEARNS STUDY, *Bibliography on Academic Dishonesty* (Boston, 1966).

RYAN, MARY P. and JOHN J. RYAN, *Life and Sexuality* (New York, 1967).

SANFORD, NEVITT, *Self and Society* (New York, 1966).
────── (ed.), *The American College* (New York, 1962).
SCHOFIELD, MICHAEL, *Sexual Behavior of Young People* (Boston, 1965).
SHAFFER, HELEN B., "Cheating in School," *Editorial Research Reports*, May 11, 1966, pp. 343–358.
SHEDD, CLARENCE P., *The Church Follows Its Students* (New Haven, 1938).
────── *Two Centuries of Student Christian Movements* (New York, 1934).
SMITH, HUSTON, *The Purposes of Higher Education* (New York, 1955).
SMITH, SEYMOUR A., *The American College Chaplaincy* (New York, 1954).
STROUP, HERBERT H., "The Touchables," *The College Experience* (San Francisco, California: California State Polytechnic College, 1962).
STUDENT COMMITTEE FOR CO-OPERATIVE EDUCATION, *Survey of Co-operative Education Student's Viewpoint* (Northeastern University, Boston, Massachusetts).
TAYLOR, NORMAN, *Narcotics: Nature's Dangerous Gifts* (New York, 1963).
TEAD, ORDWAY, *Character Building and Higher Education* (New York, 1953).
"The Morals Revolution on the U.S. Campus," *Newsweek*, LXIII:14, April 6, 1964, pp. 52–59.
THE VAN PELT CONFERENCE AT UNION COLLEGE, *Fraternities: Challenge and Opportunity* (Schenectady, 1963).
"This Is My Own Work," *Scholastic*, May 5, 1934, p. 3.
THOMAS ALVA EDISON FOUNDATION, *Co-operative Education and the Impending Educational Crisis*, 1957.
TOWNSEND, AGATHA, *College Freshmen Speak Out* (New York, 1956).
TYLER, RALPH W., and ANNICE L. MILLS, *Report on Co-operative Education* (Thomas Alva Edison Foundation, 1961).
UNGERLEIDER, J. THOMAS, and DUKE FISHER, "LSD, Research and Joy Ride," *Nation*, 202, May 16, 1966, pp. 575–576.
VON HOFFMAN, NICHOLAS, *The Multiversity* (New York, 1966).
WAGONER, WALTER D., *The Seminary—Protestant and Catholic* (New York, 1966).
WAKING, EDWARD, *The Catholic Campus* (New York, 1963).
WALLIN, J. E. W., "Literary Piracy," *School and Society*, October 18, 1930, pp. 527–529.
WALSH, CHAD, *Campus Gods on Trial* (New York, 1962).
WALTER, ERICH A., *Religion and the State University* (Ann Arbor, 1958).
WATSON, GLADYS H., *The Brooklyn College Student: A Pilgrim's Progress* (New York, 1966).
WILSON, JAMES W., and EDWARD H. LYONS, *Work-Study College Programs* (New York, 1961).

WIZE, W. MAX, *They Come For the Best of Reasons* (Washington, D.C., 1958).

WOLSELEY, ROLAND E., "Plan for Plagiarists," *Saturday Review*, May 10, 1958, p. 25.

WOOLDRIDGE, ROY L., *Student Employment and Co-operative Education* (New York, 1964).

WRENN, C. GILBERT (ed.), *College Life* (New York, 1966).

YANKOWSKI, JOHN S., *Yankowski Report on Premarital Sex* (Los Angeles, 1965).